KT-423-513

When The Feast Is Finished

A Memoir of Love and Bereavement

BRIAN ALDISS

with
Margaret Aldiss

WARNER BOOKS

A *Warner* Book

First published in Great Britain in 1999
by Little, Brown and Company
This edition published in 2000 by Warner Books

Copyright © Brian W. Aldiss 1999

The moral right of the author has been asserted.

A CIP catalogue record for this book
is available from the British Library.

ISBN 0 7515 2995 8

Typeset in Garamond by M Rules
Printed and bound in Great Britain by
Clays Ltd, St Ives plc

Warner Books
A Division of
Little, Brown and Company (UK)
Brettenham House
Lancaster Place
London WC2E 7EN

Brian Aldiss was born in East Dereham, Norfolk, in 1925. After serving with the Royal Signals in the Far East, he settled in Oxford. His first book, *The Brightfount Diaries* (1955) was based on his experiences working in one of the city's bookshops, followed two years later by his first collection of short stories, *Space, Time and Nathaniel*. He has published over fifty books, including the bestselling *The Horatio Stubbs Saga*, the Helliconia Trilogy, a critical history of science fiction, *Billion Year Spree* and *Frankenstein Unbound*, filmed in 1990.

A commendably diverse creative force, Aldiss is principally known as a writer and critic of science fiction. He has received wide acclaim for his short stories, travel writing, poetry and contemporary novels: *Life in the West* (1980) was chosen by Anthony Burgess as one of the ninety-nine best novels to have appeared since 1945. It forms the first volume of the Squire Quartet, now reissued by Abacus. Brian Aldiss's autobiography, *The Twinkling of an Eye*, was published in 1998. He continues to live in Oxford.

To Alison
Who made my life habitable
after the feast was finished –
with much gratitude

In loving memory of my wife
Margaret Christie Manson Aldiss

I called for madder music and for stronger wine.
But when the feast is finished and the lamps expire
There falls thy shadow, Cynara, the night is thine.
And I am desolate and sick of an old passion,
Yeah, hungry for the lips of my desire.
I have been faithful to thee, Cynara, in my fashion.

ERNEST DOWSON

Introduction

We must all be grateful to Brian Aldiss for his courage and determination in writing this fine book about the terminal illness of his wife, Margaret, who claimed she was not 'important' enough for such attention. In doing so, he has given us a portrait of a remarkable woman and a remarkable marriage; he has also produced the best day-to-day, personal account of a terminal illness I have ever read.

Anyone who has worked with the dying will instantly recognise the authenticity of this account, which is particularly valuable to medical professionals in its report of the first-rate hospice care provided by the Sir Michael Sobell House, Oxford. For this reason alone, the book should be read by every hospice worker and all medical and nursing students and practitioners.

For the general reader, the extraordinary honesty of the book makes it compelling reading. Brian Aldiss is an excellent writer and he writes as life really is: raw, contradictory, repetitive, bright at one moment, unbearable at the next, glorious, infuriating, ultimately mysterious beyond our power to comprehend.

I believe it is a book that will comfort many people who face similar circumstances, including the dying themselves, as well as the care-givers and the bereaved. Such a fearlessly intimate glimpse into lives in crisis serves to remind us all that whatever happens, we are not in this alone.

Sandol Stoddard
Leading advocate of
The Hospice Movement
and author of
*The Hospice Movement:
A Better Way of Caring
for the Dying.*

[I]

It was a faultless day in July, hot, sunny, and still. Margaret and I drove over to the country *pied-à-terre* of our friends Hilary and Helge Rubinstein for lunch. The Rubinsteins welcomed us with their usual warmth. Already other guests were gathering in the garden.

Hilary had set up three tables in the shade of an apple tree while Helge was preparing a lavish cold buffet. Lots of wine, white and red, stood waiting, together with mineral water and Pimms in jugs, brimming with fruit. Margaret sat at one table, I at another, and we enjoyed conversations with friends. Anthony and Catherine Storr were there. This cottage was where I had first met the Storrs, many a year ago, and we are on affectionate terms. One of Anthony's books is being translated into Korean, another into Mongolian.

Also present was Catriona Bass, a brave and elegant lady who visited Tibet shortly before Margaret went there. The Rhubras, cheerful as usual – Ben, the portrait painter, and his clever potter wife. We enjoyed the company of Philip Sievert and his new wife, Veronica. Philip is youthful and his carefully poised sentences give him an air of stateliness, as if he had emerged from a Henry James novel. On the morrow he was to start editorial work at Harvill Press. Amazingly characteristic of him.

Several other people were there, including the charming Cissy Gill. I loved them all. Perhaps the reflection occurred to me then that to grow old held its own pleasures, when the need to compete had faded and ambition had put away its armour; that to be middle class and English was not the worst of fates the world had in store; that stability was a fortunate quality which had come Margaret's and my way; and that to be sitting under that particular apple tree at that particular time with those particular acquaintances was to be rated among the good things of this world.

But the afternoon wore on, the apples slowly ripened on their tree, and I was a little anxious about Margaret. As we were leaving, I expressed a wish to Hilary that that 1997 afternoon could have gone on for ever, forever warm and golden, forever in good company.

When we got home, the sun was still blazing away as if intending to fulfil my wish. Margaret and I sat together outside in our little amphitheatre, almost purring. Despite our earlier trepidations, Margaret seemed perfectly well.

That morning, as we were preparing for the occasion, I had seen Margaret, walking slowly in the garden, sink on to a bench. Going to her, I asked her if she was well enough to face the occasion.

'I'm not sure. You know if I have to stand . . .' She smiled at me, letting the sentence trail. We both knew she had a slight heart problem, an enlarged left ventricle, which made her weak on her legs.

'I can ring Helge now and put it off. She'll understand. I'll tell her you're not well.'

'No, we'll go. I'll be all right.'

'If you feel the slightest bit rotten when we're there, just say the word and we can drive home at once.'

In truth, Margaret was far from well. I have searched my old diaries for hints of when her illness began. We spent many years living happily on Boars Hill, to the south of Oxford, where we tended a large woodland garden. The house itself was an unspoilt Edwardian building, with an unusual feature, a large living-room with clerestory windows that surveyed the rear lawns and pond. There, Margaret frequently became tired and would go to bed early, leaving me to read or watch old films on TV. It was her habit; we accepted it as part of life.

Despite her beautiful clear English voice, Margaret was a Scot, although she had been born in England, in Maidstone, Kent. The Clan Gunn, to which she belonged, hailed from the Shetland Islands. Perhaps it was this northern heritage that made her somewhat vulnerable to hot weather. In May 1995, she and I had met up with the rest of the family in the Cyclades. We stayed in the pleasant town of Naussa, on Paros, to celebrate our son Clive's fortieth birthday. It was certainly warm there; Margaret had to spend one day in our hotel, resting.

Slowly, it became apparent that she had a heart problem. This was diagnosed in September of 1995. At that time, our four children having grown up and left home, we were planning to sell our large house on Boars Hill and move to a smaller one in Old Headington. Margaret noted in a laconic diary entry:

> *I am diagnosed with heart trouble, enlarged left ventricle, owing to high blood pressure.*

Although she remained under doctor's orders, she was unable to take life as easily as we might have wished. The house we had bought, Hambleden, needed much attention, such as a complete rewiring and the ripping out of all the old pipes, which were a mixture of copper and lead. For a while, most of the floorboards in the house were up. We moved in that October, living uncomfortably while additional rooms and a new hall and staircase were added to the house, and the garden was landscaped.

It was all a serious challenge for a lady with a heart problem. I'm amazed to think back and recall how casually we were house-hunting on that summer's day when we agreed to buy the little place. But in those days we were high-spirited and relaxed together about most things.

My diary note for the 3rd of July 1996 mentions that we went out for a meal on the evening before Margaret had an angiogram.

> As we were driving home, she said, 'I know this is silly, but there's something I want to say'.
>
> What followed was, 'If anything goes wrong tomorrow, I would like to be buried here, in Headington Cemetery'. (She did not want to go alone to East Dereham.)

East Dereham was the small Norfolk town in which I had been born. In Margaret's and my palmy days, I had bought a plot adjacent to my grandfather's grave in the town cemetery. Why had I done it? As a joke? Or was I prompted by an absurd longing to return to the town I had left at the age of twelve?

Of course I heeded what Margaret said. If she wished to be buried in our local cemetery, so it should be – and I would follow her there. I tried to sell my Dereham plot to Betty, my sister living in Norfolk, but she turned down the offer. She did not think it a good idea, any more than Margaret had done.

My poor darling! This was one of her few indications of worry. In the night, I dreamed that she was driving on the wrong side of a fast road. We witnessed an accident, where it seemed that a man, possibly a cyclist, was killed; but he got up and walked away.

I drove her round to the John Radcliffe Hospital this morning. We were there before eight. She was installed on Level 5c, private ward 16. She gives me her dear sweet smile – as ever, she is calm and collected, maybe too collected. I feel that her delicacy of character permeates and informs the family. We would all be lesser people without her presence.

Although I hated to leave her, she sat on the bed, radiating confidence. Angiograms are minor exploratory ops, but hardly comfortable.

During an angiogram, a dye is inserted into the coronary arteries, so that they are clearly outlined in X-rays. It causes some discomfort and may possibly bring complications, but it does provide clear evidence of disease.

I left Margaret because I had to go to see Andy, a carpenter working on the extension of the house. The builders were with us for a year.

Later. I walked back to the hospital at 1 p.m. There was my darling, in bed, alert, looking quite rosy. The angiogram all over, with positive results. No arterial deterioration, merely an enlarged left ventricle, which could be cured by exercise and dieting. I tell her, next week we can swim in Spain.

She must lie flat, then semi-flat, and I may be able to collect her by six, and bring her back home.

Rang my sister Betty with the news.

5th July 1996
Margaret seems fine. A bruise on her groin, otherwise lovely. We're relieved, of course.

Wendy brought her some freesias.

6th July 1996
She really seems happy with the weight off her mind. We strolled round Headington and bought some art materials. Then a wardrobe for the guest room, for Clive and Youla [Clive's wife] when they arrive from Athens next month. It's Youla's birthday. We phoned her in Prigipou.

Moggins [my pet name for Margaret] now takes pleasure in organising Twinkling of an Eye [my autobiography]. Has provided excellent index. Now she separates chapters, in preparation for submitting disks to publisher. As ever, we work amiably together.

Walking about in the sun, we admit to each other that we don't relish the day, sure to come, when we can no longer stroll about the world freely, as now.

At this time we were light-hearted, happy in each other's company. Nevertheless, we were under some strain. The builders, good though they were, were constantly about us. Until the new study was built on to the north of the house,

Margaret and I operated in a small room, each with our computers on our desks, crunched together in a space eight by fourteen feet. The enlarged ventricle seemed a small matter, curable by cutting down on cream teas in Norfolk, by walking daily to the shops and bank.

I wonder now why we were so carefree, why we purchased with hardly a thought a house which initially caused us so much trouble and expense. Well, houses in Oxford were hard to come by but, above that, we enjoyed each other's company, found life fun, and did not think much beyond the day. And we took it for granted that I, six years Margaret's senior, would die first.

So our mainly sunny life continued, with trips to Spain, Portugal and Greece. This last Greek visit was in May 1997. Before we left England, we had had some anxieties regarding the heat factor and Margaret's energies. Our problems were eased by Clive and Youla who, ensconced in Athens, made many preparations which smoothed our way.

After relaxing on the island of Aegina with Clive and Youla, we headed northwards, to the Meteora, which we had been hoping to visit ever since the mid-sixties, and then into the wilder northern Greece. Northern Greece is very different from the Classical Greece which existed to the south; here one traffics with the ghost of Byzantium, where several transitory tinpot empires ruled. When we arrived in Thessaloniki, Margaret was tired, although still game. I booked us a room in the Elektra Palace Hotel in Aristotelious Square, looking out to sea. 'Delighted to see how happy the touch of luxury made dear Moggins', says the journal I kept. 'Perhaps the journey – this gorgeous idle journey! – has been a bit tough on her.'

Now I see how she felt unwell much of the time, saying nothing. She became impatient with my *nostalgie de la boue* at one point. We were strolling in a quieter part of Thessaloniki, as far as there is a quieter part, when we saw a pretty side street in which pseudo-acacias grew on the pavement. A little rickety hotel stood in the street. If you took a room up on the sixth floor, high above the pedestrians, you could stand on a balcony with green railings and look out on sun and the tops of the trees. It was so romantic, I longed to be there.

Saying as much started an argument. Margaret said we were too old for that kind of thing. It would be a sordid little room, up too many steps. We needed comfort at our age.

She was right. It might have been squalid up there, perched in a cheap Greek hotel. Her diary reports the incident thus:

B goes on about small romantic hotels in crummy side
streets. I finally shut him up, saying I'm not up to
travelling that way any more. We argue. It's unusual.
Later, as a gesture, he buys me a pretty candle.

Although I found nothing to complain about, and much to interest us, I was not ill. Now I'm sorry I did not see how little she enjoyed the northern part of the trip.

'You must think I'm an awful person to take out,' she says. She smiles and takes her supper pill. She has left her food again, as invariably she does. She has the appetite of a sparrow.

Privately, she had more serious complaints. Her diary entry for the 14th of May reads:

*Dreadful night, noisy music from lobby, noisy lorries
setting off up hill, wild dogs barking in garden. And an
empty stomach. This is something of an endurance feat
and I will never agree to another trip with such
hardships – Greece is such a difficult place.*

It comes hard to acknowledge that my responses were so different. My journal speaks quite fondly of the hotel we were in at this time. It was called the Hotel King Alexander, and stood on a hill on well-kept grounds just outside the city of Florina. As well as the customary Greek flag, the hotel flew EU and Australian flags. We were installed in Room 104. I report it as being clean and comfortable, with a balcony, overlooking the red-roofed outer town and the mountains. I note that Margaret was pleased with it.

I was writing my notes out on the balcony at dusk. Dogs were barking in the hills and a bird occasionally gave out one beautiful liquid note. The scent of lilac lingered in the air. I wrote, in my naïve way:

I adore – am excited by – Florina. The plump little lady in the
pizza restaurant speaks a few words of English, and I'm pleased.

Now I'm sad to see that Margaret suffered so much in May 1997. Our holidays abroad had always been pleasurable for her. Clearly the cancer was already surreptitiously working to make her miserable.

Margaret spoke longingly of the isle of Bornholm, in the Baltic,
'where people are civilised and food is good.' 'And,' I said, 'it's

windy and cold'. Here in our room, she, smiling, says, 'You're
content wherever you are.'

And content nowhere without her.

On Greece's northern frontier with Macedonia, she
bought herself a pack of little bottles of Unterberg, 'natural
herb bitters taken for digestion'. It was uncharacteristic of
her. She made a joke of it, and I swigged a bottle with her.

This account stands as an example of male insensitivity. It
is also an example of Margaret's self-effacement. She was 'a
good sport'; she tried not to spoil other people's enjoyment.
At this period, neither of us knew that a more sinister and
lethal ill than her enlarged ventricle was creeping up on her.
And she looked so well . . .

Back in England, summer was upon us. Our house was
finished, our garden was landscaped, our waterfall was tink-
ling away. We sat in our pleasing paved helix outside the
house, doing very little. Margaret read gardening books and
nursed Sotkin. We had two cats, the second being Macramé,
but kindly, furry Sotkin, was her treasure. Perhaps she needed
his comfort as he obviously needed hers.

Although I was writing my utopia, *White Mars*, in collaboration with Sir Roger Penrose, I now worked fewer hours.
When I bumped into my neighbour Harry Brack, we went
and drank coffee and conversed in the Café Noir. When I
returned to Margaret, she said, 'That's just the sort of thing
you should be doing, now that you're retired.'

But. I find it is one thing to sit and talk over coffee with
a friend when you can go home to your wife, and quite
another when you can't, when there's no wife. Who wants

to talk in those circumstances? I would rather be alone, *skulking*.

Our last summer drifted by. It was on the 20th of July we enjoyed that happy lunch with the Rubinsteins in their garden.

But on the following day, Margaret wrote to our GP, Dr Neil MacLennan, asking for another appointment with Dr Hart, her cardiologist, whom she had been consulting since September 1995. On that occasion my diary says:

> My peachy creature had to go to the cardiologist, Mr Hart (sic), for examination. She gets short of breath. The diagnosis: the walls of her heart are too thick, while slight blood pressure affects the situation. More tests to come.
>
> She displayed no anxiety before the examination. I concealed my anxiety. Afterwards she appeared smiling and calm as usual.
>
> Following Mr Hart's advice, we'll now be careful about diet, to protect the tender walls of that tender heart. No more cream teas, jam roly-polys, pork pies, etc. . . . A part of me regards myself as indestructible; another part admits the truth – about both of us . . .

One cannot resist searching through old notebooks for indications one ignored, warnings to which a blind eye had been turned. For instance, during that last summer in Woodlands, on Boars Hill, Margaret was under the weather. Hardly surprising. It was the third hottest August since records began.

'My dear wife wilts', says the diary on the 3rd.

On the 10th, she went into the Acland, Oxford's private hospital, for a colonoscopy, under Mr Kettlewell. When I went in to see her, she was enjoying a light meal and was in bonny spirits. She always made so little fuss. On the following day, when she was back home, I took her her breakfast in bed, and she had a gentle day. On the 16th, we drove up to Stratford-on-Avon to see Vanbrugh's *The Relapse* or 'Virtue in Danger', and laughed heartily.

During this hectic time, we were endeavouring to sell our Boars Hill house and to prepare the place in Old Headington for human habitation.

And why did we sell up, after eleven happy years on Boars Hill? To leave was originally Margaret's idea. She explained that we were growing older and feebler. Her diaries of the time indicate that I was rather unwell and working under stress, at least in her opinion. There were many old Boars Hill couples living deteriorating lives in deteriorating housing; she did not wish us to follow the same downward path. She was finding the tending of her long flowerbed beyond her. Soon the pruning and lopping of borders would be beyond me.

Slowly I warmed to her plan. One of the few shortcomings of Boars Hill was that one could walk nowhere. Not down into Wootton or, in the other direction, down to the Abingdon Road and Oxford. We had to use the car to get anywhere. After much searching, we bought the house in Old Headington and began slowly to clear out the possessions we had accumulated on the hill.

The move has proved to be an excellent decision. Did Margaret have an intuition of the illness that was to kill her in two years' time? I am convinced this was the case, at least in part. If not, then it was Margaret's good sense. We needed to live in a simpler place.

Margaret disputed the role of intuition in our move into town. However, understandings arise from our bodies and seep into consciousness by devious paths which science may one day come to understand. During our last months in Woodlands and our first few months in Hambleden, I developed a phobia of finding a snake about the house, more particularly the all-devouring anaconda. I tried to turn this fear into a joke; Margaret was not happy with it. The all-devouring one was lurking in the dark. Probably she was already in its coils.

Yet we remained happy and carefree, as far as that was possible. We were of that fortunate few for whom being happy had become a habit. On my birthday in 1996, the 18th of August, Margaret's present to me was the newly published two-volume set of Claire Clairmont's *Correspondence*. She read the letters with me.

We had received an offer for the purchase of Woodlands, and we threw a party – a farewell party it was to be. A band of musicians calling themselves 'The Skeleton Crew' played baroque music until late. Our local caterers, the Huxters, served gorgeous food, and sixty of our friends attended. Margaret was a wonderful hostess, looking slender and lovely. No one could suspect there was anything troubling her.

During the evening, I persuaded her to stroll with me downhill to the bottom of the rear lawn. We looked back. There in the dark, like a ship, sailed our house, its windows alight, full of family, friends, food, drink and happiness: something we had conjured up together.

And when the guests had departed, Tim and I sat peacefully together and finished up what remained of an excellent Brie.

At the end of that memorable August, Margaret and I were in Glasgow, celebrating with the Fifty-Third World SF Convention, which took over the entire vast SECC building. Something like twelve thousand people had subscribed to the event. This was the great family of SF fandom's annual festivity. Among those present from overseas were Sam and Ingrid Lundwall from Sweden and Marcial Souto from Argentina. Margaret and Ingrid, good friends, went shopping together in Glasgow.

Marcial had once worked with Jorges Luis Borges. We've known each other since 1970. Conversations with him, as with Sam, rank among the pleasures of this life.

In this crowded time, Margaret remained sunny and optimistic, as my diary reports.

Monday 9th October 1995. The week when we MUST leave Woodlands. The removal vans come tomorrow. M and I have ordered our lives well and sensibly of recent years, thanks to her organising skills; we often feel this move to Headington is our big mistake. Jock MacGregor [our decorator] reassured her yesterday: 'In a week or two you'll have a lovely house.'

The whole matter is occasioned by our growing old and my books failing to find an audience. Best thing is to accept the situation and get on with it: as Margaret valiantly does.

So we left Woodlands and moved into the Old Headington house, in which our plumber was busy laying over four hundred metres of new copper piping.

Standing in the front of No. 39, lo and behold! , I suddenly
espied both of my beautiful daughters strolling along, coming
to see how we were getting on!

Both Wendy and Charlotte were as ever very close to us, and
to each other. How fortunate we have been that our four children, Clive and Wendy (Margaret's step-children) Tim and
Charlotte, are peaceable people, and that we all enjoy each
other's company. One expression of our closeness was the
family's fondness of nicknames. Margaret called Tim *Booj*,
while she herself was called *Chris* by Clive, Wendy and
Wendy's husband, Mark. Charlotte's name had somehow
become shortened to *Chagie*. And at one time, my sister
Betty was known as *Big Aunt Rose* . . .

It's a wonder that we survived the housing upheaval. We
were both exhausted. Margaret was hardly able to take the
rest periods recommended. The cardiologist's analysis of
Margaret's condition was that the enlarged left ventricle of
her heart was causing her shortness of breath. There was also
some bacterial damage to the top part of the aorta. Her blood
pressure was high.

It's very upsetting. But Moggins remains so calm I hardly
know how much to be alarmed. We got some prescribed pills
from Hornby's, the Headington pharmacy, during the day.

If one has to become ill, Oxford is an excellent city to do
it in. It is well equipped with medical experts and efficient
hospitals. We were to find that our new home was conve-
niently situated for visiting clinics, cardiologists, and those

elements of a more ominous regime, oncologists and hospices. But for a while we seemed able to lead a stable life. With the aid of our GP, the heart trouble could be controlled, even improved. Margaret needed more rest; then she would be better.

Of course, rest with builders on the premises is hard to come by. Nor were we particularly expert in the subject of rest.

In 1996, I made six brief trips abroad as usual, and turned down offers of several more. On a few of these expeditions Margaret accompanied me, for instance to Madeira, Spain and Portugal. Unfortunately, she could not come with me on the most memorable visit, to Israel, on the grounds that it would be too hot for her there.

I cannot claim I was particularly well myself; sometimes I travelled because I felt an obligation to do so – although this was not so in the case of Israel. I missed Margaret on that interesting visit – indeed, I missed her as soon as I was on the El Al plane, finding I had no credit cards with me! One of my kind hosts at the Tel Aviv British Council, Mrs Sonia Feldman, trustingly lent me her credit card.

Turning up a journal I kept of the days in Israel, I find my first entry, made on the plane, reads:

I'm alone. M and I were due to make the trip, but she is too frail and unwell. She makes light of her troubles, but it's worrying; her cardiac weakness remains a problem. She thinks too that dust from the building site (our extension is now well under way) causes her breathing problems. It may well be so.

It's a sadness to see how much less lively she has become in the six months since we left our lovely Woodlands.

The cancer must have been at its destructive secret work, a sapper undermining her being. It is useless to curse oneself for not looking beyond the heart trouble. But one does.

Our visit to Cascais, on the Portuguese coast, was not really a success, kind though our hosts were. This was Portugal's first international science fiction convention/conference. The occasion was very important for the organisers and they had persuaded us to go.

Go we did, despite many difficulties. We had planned to travel on from Cascais to visit Lisbon for a holiday. Friendly people met us at the airport on the Wednesday. But, on the morning of Sunday the 29th of September, I woke to find Margaret very weepy, quite unlike her usual self. She said she was feeling ill and her heart was overtaxed by heat, standing about and difficult food.

Margaret had never been a moody person. I was alarmed. At once I said that we'd better get back into the cool and the damp, and forget about Lisbon. I immediately cancelled everything, including our stay in the plush Lisbon hotel, and we returned home that evening.

On the following day, I report with relief that

Margaret is fine again – 'right as rain'. The rain, the cold, the cloud of England, seem to suit her best. No standing about, no having to talk to people.

But she was in truth far from fine, as she recorded.

I woke feeling bad, fast heartbeats, very dry nose and eyes, cold feet. Told B who said we should go home today. I

*burst into tears . . . instead of keeping a stiff upper lip as
usual. I had not admitted even to myself what an ordeal
these events often are, esp. in heat and having to stand
around. B so busy and preoccupied.*

This entry made sad reading after her death. I could but
curse myself for seeming neglectful. Yet only two pages earlier, in Margaret's neat little A6 diary, I read of a happier
mood.

*Bus trip to Sintra. Went along the coast to westernmost
point of Europe, Cabo de Roca. So dramatic, with
Atlantic waves pouring in, crashing on great cliffs.
   Sintra Palace was closed. It's a pretty rundown hilltop
town, being restored, full of souvenirs. Good company on
the bus . . . Into town for a meal on our own . . . Rice and
seafood, quite good, 'flan' even better. Then to theatre where
B gave his talk to a good audience. Audience laughed
immoderately at B's remarks. He was funny and good, but
not that funny! Projected slides of his book covers looked
good. Then twenty or so of us took over the centre of a tiny
street and sat talking until 12.30. Still warm at midnight.*

That was on the Friday. What was plaguing her on the
Sunday must have been the undiscovered cancer and not
solely the heart problem, to which we ascribed her sorrows.
There was no reason to believe that something worse assailed
her. Perhaps we might have been more suspicious had we
been better versed in medical matters.

   And she took care in that little notebook to worry about

my trivial problems. She writes on the Thursday (26th of September):

> *Poor B, with bad legs, took ¾ pain-killer last night, which gave him a good sleep but left him very blotto this morning. (We had been to hospital and doctor about his health on Tuesday – he is nervous about his stomach and how he will cope – doctor assures us there are no life-threatening troubles, though.) I also suffer from my heart condition and lack of resistance to heat and cold.*

We both became ill once we were established at home. I generally got up first, went downstairs, fed the cats, and took us up mugs of tea to begin the day. On 21st of October, I felt bad enough to remain in bed.

Lovely still sunny morning. Being in the bedroom, I'm privileged to see Margaret dress and 'do her face' – the morning ritual. A modest and charming ritual, sitting at her modest dressing table.

Hers is about the pleasantest face I ever set eyes on, as she is certainly the pleasantest woman. She works hard: the shopping, the cooking, the house-cleaning, much gardening, our financial affairs; and just now the seemingly endless retyping of *Twinkling*.

This week, she'll drive down to Bath to see Chagie and will buy herself a large new loom.

All her activity, her travelling, her weaving, hardly indicated an invalid. Nor did she regard herself as an invalid.

I may have taken the many things Margaret so cheerfully did for granted, but I never took her for granted. I had had a taste of worse things, and rejoiced in my good fortune and her delightful presence. On the 22nd of October:

Ill or not, our days here pass pleasantly with the two of us together. They could continue thus for many a year and I'd be happy. We had the additional pleasure this afternoon of Wendy's company for a couple of hours. She sat on the *chaise longue* in our (new) study, and chatted amiably of her plans, which include buying a seaside cottage at Morthoe.

While Wendy was here, Harry [Harrison] rang. He attended the memorial service for Kingsley [Amis], to which I was too under the weather to go. There he had the pleasure of seeing Hilly and Jane exchange a kiss.

With Margaret's aid, I despatched the final version of *The Twinkling of an Eye* to HarperCollins, then my publisher. Life went on light-heartedly. Margaret enjoyed the literary life, with its struggles and excitements. She had perhaps had early preparation for it, since a book had been dedicated to her when she was a small girl. This sweet little book, of which ours must be one of the few surviving copies, is *Bubble and the Circus*, written and illustrated by Josephine Hatcher. It was published by the now defunct firm of Hollis & Carter, in 1946.

Margaret and I had known each other for forty years, and had been married for most of them. We had not always been as absorbed in one another as was later the case. We had both taken other lovers, brief joys that are followed by the storms of jealousy and fury which such events generally bring. Although I am not without regret that we behaved then as we did, I can see it as an episode in our maturing process. When we were reconciled, we became more dear to one another.

We drove down to Brighton, where Tim worked, met up with him, and dined with Marina Warner and a jolly crowd after the opening of Marina's exhibition, 'The Inner Eye', in which I took part. Meanwhile, I began to make plans for *White Mars* with Sir Roger Penrose. Roger and his wife Vanessa had bought Woodlands, whereupon we became friends.

On the 11th of December in that year, 1996, Moggins and I celebrated our thirty-first wedding anniversary. We had no inkling that it was to be our last anniversary. Nevertheless, there were discomforts.

My dear faithful and true wife and I hug and kiss each other, and rejoice. We warmly remember that happy day of our marriage, and the celebrations in the Randolph Hotel with all our charming friends present. Plus the flight to Paris after, and the plush double bed in the Scandic Hotel.

But – Margaret's celebrating with an hour in Stephen Henderson's [our dentist's] chair. She has to have a crown removed. Because of her heart condition, she had to take penicillin first thing. I shall go and collect her in half an hour.

By the 17th of December I report Margaret as being 'almost over her little dental op'. Christmas was on the way. She was cooking mince-pies, and preparing to serve Christmas dinner for the whole family, as she had been doing for many a year.

Malcolm Edwards, my editor at HarperCollins, had by now had the typescript of *Twinkling* for two weeks, and uttered no word on the subject. My American literary agent, Robin Straus, phoned though, full of praise and excitement regarding *Twinkling* – 'A unique book – I know of no autobiography like it', etc., etc. Good.

Margaret and I gave each other a Macintosh Performa 6400/200 for Christmas. We had not yet emerged from our Mad About Computers stage.

On the last day of 1996, my spirits seem to have been low, to judge by the diary entry.

> A low grade year. Margaret's sad heart problem, the long drag of having this building enlarged, the drab political situation, the sorrow of BSE and slaughter of so many cattle, and so on . . . The hell with the boring Eurosceptics.
>
> Let's hope next year will be better! For one thing, *Twinkling* will be published, although already I dread the insensitive reviews with their crass headlines, 'Life of Brian'. But a little welcome income might trickle in.
>
> Clive and I drove down to BBC Thames Valley, where I went on air with Colin Dexter in a New Year Resolution Show. Uri Geller said he wished everyone to get down on their knees and pray for peace in the Middle East. I suggested, 'Why not try bending a few Kalashnikovs? It might be more effective.'

I failed to note down, but still vividly remember, Margaret saying, 'I don't like the sound of 1997. I don't think it is going to be the best of years . . .' Intuition again?

After the difficulties of the previous year, I made a resolution to accept no more invitations to other countries, although my customary visit to the US remained on the agenda. It was as well I did so. The temptation most difficult to resist was an invitation from Yang Xiao, one of our powerful friends in China, to a conference taking place in Beijing and Changdu. China – and indeed that remarkable lady – always had a special place in my heart.

Unlike our usual bouncy state, we were depressed in January 1997. Margaret developed a persistent sore throat. But we smiled and said, 'So this is what growing old is like!' At least we were content together; the old assumption still prevailed, that I would die first, while Margaret had at least twenty more years of life to run.

By the end of the month, I heard from Robin Straus that my American publisher, Gordon Van Gelder of St Martin's Press, 'adored' *Twinkling*. He accepted it without talk of cuts or fussing. Still there came no word from HarperCollins.

So the year began dismally. Daughter Wendy's little son, Thomas, had sickness problems, Antony, my sister Betty's husband, was asthmatic and had difficulties with food, Betty was on pills, and Moggins was definitely under par. She stayed at home while I had to attend various events in England on my own. I also went to the John Radcliffe for a spell under the Magnetic Resonance Scanner. Taking a look afterwards at the shots of my spine, I saw that most vertebrae were well padded and separated, but some of the lower ones were a bit shaky. They could be causing the leg pain I was experiencing.

Until I referred back to my diary, I had forgotten that things weren't so good at that time. Unwell or not, we enjoyed each other's companionship. In the evenings, after supper, we sat and read or watched television, too lacking in energy to go out.

I had a little excitement to spur me on. Sir Crispin Tickell, then the Warden of Green College, had invited me to lecture as final speaker in a series of four lectures on the future. I spoke as the president of a largely fictitious body, APIUM, the Association for the Protection and Integrity of an Unspoilt Mars. It pleased me that *apium* was the Latin word for a white vegetable, celery. I had become sensitive to the vulnerability of things, from the quiet decency of most English people, the cultivation of truth and learning in our children, to the sacredness of environments, as well as Margaret's health. Beauty lay everywhere, even on our desolate neighbouring planet, Mars.

My argument was that while I was eager for mankind to visit Mars and explore it, plans to terraform it were a different matter. Terraforming seeks to change a planet into a semblance of Earth, with breathable atmosphere, better climate, etc. Such engineering dreams are an extreme example, however well meaning, of mankind's disastrous ambition to dominate the world, to exert power, to 'conquer' every environment.

Margaret's environment was itself under threat. And I was planning to build a utopia . . . I spoke feelingly at Green College concerning this hypothetical just society, and was well received by the learned audience. Happily, Margaret was in the hall with friends, looking marvellous in a long red costume. One of the friends was the literary agent Felicity Bryan. Someone asked her after the talk, 'Was Brian an actor?'

Felicity's response: 'You mean you haven't seen *SF Blues*?' *SF Blues* was my evening revue, which I had been touring round England and abroad for a number of years, taking the leading role. We staged it once in Felicity's and her husband Alex's grand house.

Following my lecture we then dined in the college, in the Tower of the Four Winds.

Gill Lustgarten reported next day that at lunch everyone talked of me and my theories. 'There was nothing else to talk about.'

All this was beneficial for serotonin levels. Margaret and I drove over to Woodstock and bought a table and six chairs for the dining-room. Having blown over £2,000, we celebrated with lunch at the Feathers. Margaret ate soup and fishcake, I tsatsiki and chorizo, followed by parfait of duck.

We seemed to be on an even keel again.

Margaret is much better in health now, although her throat still troubles her. She looks very neat. Her legs and ankles are as slender as they were when we first met.

We drove to our flat in Blakeney on the north Norfolk coast in February, with Margaret at the wheel, and enjoyed a little sunshine. In Holt, we visited Betty and Antony's new home in Mill Street, decorated in the Victorian manner.

For a brief while, we were able to enjoy life, without realising how precious those last months were. On the day Deng Xiaoping died, we went to London to see the Braque exhibition at the Royal Academy, of which we were members. We viewed some of the canvases with almost religious reverence, as did many of the people in the galleries. After lunch, we went to see Kenneth Branagh's *Hamlet*, filmed at Blenheim

Palace. Branagh, far from being a melancholy Dane, acted more like an escapee from a military band.

The weather was awful that day.

At this stage, we worried slightly, but nothing more. We had grown accustomed to each other's weaknesses. So much so that – with the usual misgivings – I went as usual to Florida, to the Conference of the Fantastic, where I have a particular title, Special Permanent Guest. I rang Margaret from the conference hotel, to hear that beautiful voice answering me from Blakeney. On that occasion, she had lunched with Betty and Antony in Holt. She sounded spry and cheerful.

With April, I made a determined attempt to garden: more particularly, to grow us some vegetables. Along came a period of fine dry weather to encourage us. London was hotter than Athens for a time. Margaret also gardened and planted four trees on the farther lawn.

While I edited an anthology of mini-sagas, following the *Daily Telegraph* competition, our energy levels seemed to have improved. This despite the drab news from my agent, Mike Shaw, that HarperCollins, like a laundry that refuses to take in washing, was not making offers for any more books just at present.

> The happier turn life has recently taken and the recovery from our transplantation to Old Headington have restored my abilities to a large extent.

So I noted. We were easily reassured that all was pretty well with us.

We drove to Blakeney again, where it was cold. There, one

night, we saw the Hale-Bopp comet blazing away into the future over the North Sea. Two weeks later, we took a weekend off at the other end of the country, holidaying with Clive and Youla, over from Greece, in a snug little hotel on Exmoor.

But Margaret's problems continued.

After her death, I found on her computer her own report on the difficulties she experienced.

How characteristic that she headed it

My health:
Following increased breathlessness this year, especially
noticeable in Greece in May in the heat, I went to Neil
MacLennan to ask for it to be investigated. My blood
pressure was diagnosed as slightly high, following a
random twenty-four-hour test several years ago, and I
have been on Adalat Retard ever since.

Neil sent me to Dr Hart in the cardiology dept. of the
J.R. I went in last week, and first was tested on the exercise
machine, the 'treadmill'. Unsurprisingly to me, I did very
badly – as Dr Hart commented – and lasted only three
mins at the first speed, and barely another three at the next
speed: a quick uphill walking pace. Then I had an echo
cardiogram, when my heartbeat was diagnosed on a screen;
then a blood test, and then an appointment for a kidney
scan later in the month (since one of the family – Tim –
has had kidney problems). I had to do a twenty-four-hour
urine sample, which I took in the next day.

Then I had a chat with Dr Hart. He told me the
results of all the tests so far, and said that I had
substantial thickening of the wall of the left ventricle –

the part of the heart responsible for pumping the blood round the body. Probably this was due to high blood pressure: although my blood pressure was not too high taken against the average blood pressure, it might be too high for me. So the thing is to tackle it more aggressively. He also recommended taking more exercise, and not lifting anything heavy at the moment.

A week later I saw MacLennan, who had heard from Dr Hart in a long letter. He gave all the results – why is it the patient is the only person not to have anything down in writing about his or her condition? That is why I am recording this! – and suggested going on to Ace Inhibitors, together with a slight diuretic, low dose to start, then increased slightly, and to see how it went.

So I took half a Enalapril last night, and had a really good relaxed sleep! With all the house moving, it is hard to be unexerted at present, but I don't feel too bad today at all. The Adalat Retard did very well for me, controlling the increased heart rate as I could feel, and also removing most headaches and nosebleeds. Interesting. Let's see what Enalapril will do.

November: Now on 10mg. Enalapril, as well as Bendofluazine. And Premarin, and doing well, though really not up to walking uphill yet. Due for a check up with Dr Hart some time soon.

March: Summoned to see Neil MacLennan because my cholesterol level was up to 11 again – 7 would be good, 5 is average . . . He proposed to put me on more pills. I said I'd rather try lowering it by improving my diet, so we agreed on that. Not due to see Dr Hart until October, but don't really feel my heart condition has improved. So I have written direct to him to ask for an appointment. I want to know why he thinks I have this condition – what it is due to. I mentioned my struggling dreams, which I have had for some years. Prior to that, in the days of Heath House and Dr Tobin (whom I told about this) I had dreams fairly often of being in some transport which was going too fast round a corner, to the extent that I nearly blacked out with the G pressure. May be related . . .

To see Dr Hart, for the six-month check-up I requested. He suggests I have an angiograph done, a tube inserted into the veins, to see if he can find out what is wrong with the blood supply. Sounds horrid, but must be done, a day in the hospital with local anaesthetic. Ugh. I have to go on to anti-cholesterol pills, to lower it. OK, maybe that will help. I await a date.

Angiogram duly done, early July: great result – no coronary artery problems at all. So, only the blood pressure and enlarged ventricle to look after, with pills, as before. Thank goodness for that!

Margaret was a great counter of blessings.

Often in the night she would wake, and then I would wake, and we would walk about the house holding hands. We put no lights on. A street lamp outside the front door filtered light into the rooms. We were always kind and fond. I enjoyed those waking times; sometimes I would fetch her a little glass of milk from the fridge.

I would hold her and kiss her. We told each other that, now we were getting old, we needed less sleep. Indeed, it was difficult to distinguish the natural pains of growing old from more serious pains, or a sense of feeling old from a sense of feeling ill. It seemed then that we were both 'getting on a bit', and so we were inclined to regard Margaret's heart problem as part of a process in which we were both involved.

Nevertheless, there was a new development. For several years, I had been taking a post-lunch siesta in the study, whereas Margaret said she could not sleep during the day. Now she began to rest on the sofa in the living-room, her beloved cat Sotkin beside her, and often would sleep for a whole hour or possibly more.

She could not think herself well again.

It was on the 14th of April that Margaret wrote the letter to her cardiologist.

Dear Dr Hart,

I came to see you in October last year, and we discovered that I have an enlarged left ventricle. I gather from my GP, Neil MacLennan, that I am not due to see you again for a year, but I really would be glad to have another appointment with you now. I don't know whether I should make it direct with you, but in any case I am sending Neil a copy of this letter.

It seems to me that things are really not much better, and I am disappointed I suppose – you said it could be 'cured', and I hoped for good things. But I still get short of breath

*very easily, and tired, and find I am not up to doing a great
deal of gardening, for instance – by which I mean digging
up shrubs and transplanting them, carting round bags of
manure, restoring our newly acquired garden, etc.!*

*I have had regular appointments with my GP, and my
blood pressure is reasonably normal; but my cholesterol
level is very high at present. I have chosen to improve my
diet rather than go on more pills, since I am aware the
diet has slipped over the winter. I have the odd 'pale day',
after a night when my heart seems to have been extra
cramped up, and then I feel unable to be particularly
active – this is something I have experienced over a few
years. I would also like to discuss with you why I have
this condition, something I really didn't ask your opinion
about. It seems to me I have trouble at night, and again
over the years I have had 'struggling' dreams which wake
me, it seems, on purpose to get my breath back. Anyway,
I am worrying about it at present and would be glad of a
check-up with you.*

I have found a note written in Margaret's elegant hand,
dated the 2nd of May 1997. It reads mysteriously: '*7.2 chol.
Liver slightly abnormal. Neil lipid doc*'.

During this period, of the early summer, we tried to live as
normal and enjoy our usual pleasures. These included our
contacts with countries overseas. A party of musicians came
to Britain from Turkmenistan to play. They performed in
the Holywell Music Room in Oxford. In the programme
interval, I was presented with a hand-woven rug into
which was woven the name of the Central Asian poet

Makhtumkuli, together with my name. This was by way of honouring my versification in English of Makhtumkuli's poems, first started when I was in Turkmenistan in 1995.

On the following day, Youssef Azemoun, the great unsung ambassador of all things Turkmen in this country, came to tea with Margaret and me. He brought with him two Turkmen ladies, Mai Canarova, a descendant of the eighteenth-century poet, and Orazgul Annamyrat, a pianist trained in the Moscow Conservatory.

Margaret served tea in the garden, in the helix. Afterwards, Orazgul came inside and played to us (Margaret was delighted she had just had the piano tuned). She had a clear attacking style, beautiful both to hear and to watch and was a remarkable person who briefly entered our lives, very friendly and quick. She quite won our hearts.

That May, as reported, Margaret and I flew to Greece for a holiday. To begin with, we took life easy, staying on Aegina in the House of Peace with Clive and Youla. We had had some concern about the heat, which was why we went early in the month.

We were back home in time for Moggins's birthday on the 23rd of May. It was to prove her last birthday.

In the middle of June, Margaret and I opened the garden to the Friends of Old Headington, and many amiable people wandered round our garden and others nearby. Among them were Jeremy and Margaret Potter. Jeremy, brave and jovial, announced that he was dying of cancer, hale and hearty though he looked. Moggins too looked so bonny that day, and radiated happiness. Yet we both knew that she was under par, and feeling weak.

On the 4th of July, we drove out to Kidlington – well, Margaret drove us to Kidlington; she usually did all the driving – to a dinner party under the hospitable roof of our friends Felicity and Alex Duncan and children. We always looked forward to visiting them. I suppose about sixteen or more people sat down to dine in their hall. During the first course, Margaret, who was sitting down the table from me, rose, and excused herself; she said she was feeling unwell. Anxiously, I went outside with her, into the cool dark. She said her heart was bothering her, and her pulse was fluttering; I was to stay and enjoy myself, because she would be fine once she got home and could lie down.

Her casual manner in part reassured me. I went to the car with her, protesting that I would go with her. No, no, she would be fine. I must go back to the party; she was sorry to leave, etc.

So I went back, but was too anxious to remain at table. I told Alex I would have to leave. Alex came with me into the night, and saw me into a taxi. I believe that that was the first moment when my anxiety broke through into full consciousness and I realised that my wife might be seriously ill.

So, while Margaret underwent various tests, still centring on her heart problem and cholesterol levels, we still tried to live as we normally did, enjoying the summer, the garden, and our orderly little house. And, of course, continuing *White Mars*.

We had both been reading *Anna Karenina* in different editions. I enjoyed the fateful love affair; Margaret, impatient with Anna, was more sympathetic to Levin's dealings with his serfs, and his love of the countryside.

I wrote my wife a letter at this period:

Tolstoy says that Levin and Kitty, during the early years of
their marriage, wrote each other two or three notes every day.
They did this even though they were constantly together, as
we are.

It seems a good idea! So I send you a little note for a
change.

I go on to thank her for her assistance in getting together the
sprawling manuscript of *Twinkling*, saying that there must be
passages in it which were not agreeable to her; nevertheless,
she did not complain or attempt to act as censor. I admired
her restraint and thanked her.

To this I received a bouncy answer. It must stand against
the criticisms of my behaviour I happened across later, which
we will come to. Meanwhile, her letter is worth quoting in
full, as proof of her affectionate and optimistic outlook on
life. And on her husband, for that matter . . .

Hello my darling,
    You sent me a lovely note at the end of last year, and
it's about time I answered it!
    We don't write to each other much these days, do we?
But we do express our love in so many happy ways, and
in our support for each other. I am so grateful for your
care and concern when my heart seems to play up and
make me rather feeble. And I am very worried about the
state of your legs — let's hope the tests and X-rays will show
up what is causing the pain. Soon, the weather will make

life easier for us, when we can get out and move around, and get more exercise in the garden.

I wish Malcolm would come through with some decent enthusiasm for your autobiography. It is such a wonderfully wide-ranging book, so much experience in it, and so many areas of life included. We will weather the curiosity of our family and friends, who will no doubt appreciate that we have survived many awful times and yet stuck together, knowing that we are the foundation of a great family structure! Lucky old us! And thank goodness for Gordon Van Gelder!

I suppose it's true and inevitable that we seem to have aged a bit over the last year, with the traumas of moving and building. I hope we will manage to enjoy the garden this year, and that you won't be too exhausted with too much travel. We'll try to have some good adventures of the easy kind!

Love you hugely as always, huge hugs – Your Moggins

Well, we did stay and try to enjoy the garden, and I did not travel abroad. Unfortunately, our Tolstoyan correspondence progressed no further, as her sorrows overtook us.

During the summer, I gave my Moggins Lisa St Aubin de Teran's autobiographical book *The Hacienda*. She was absorbed by it, and by Lisa's terrible life, and wanted to read more of her writing. She lent The *Hacienda* to Betty, who also devoured it.

Friends I had met originally at the Conference of the Fantastic, Gary Wolfe and Dede Weil – now married – were in Europe. They had said they wished to see England beyond London, so Margaret and I planned a short trip for them. It was to prove our last carefree little excursion, and the most valued because of it, for all four of us.

Margaret drove me from Oxford to Tiverton Parkway, a smart little railway halt in the West Country. She seemed in good health again, although it was no surprise when she stayed sitting in the car while I went to the platform to meet our guests. They had come down from London by train, to save them a long car journey.

The weather was beautiful. The four of us drove down to Tarr Steps, where the river flows shallowly through a deep valley. A low stone bridge, little grander than a giant's stepping stones, crosses the river. Adults paint there, children pretend to fall in. There we stayed for a night, enjoying each other's company. Gary is witty and humane; Dede is intense, empathetic and affectionate. Time for Dede is rendered particularly special because she has suffered from cancer, has had one lung removed, and has lived to tell the tale.

On the following day, we moved to a more comfortable hotel, the Royal Oak in Winsford. Margaret and Dede drove to Winsford; Gary and I walked up a leafy valley, past a herd of the semi-wild Exmoor ponies, through countryside that has scarcely changed since before Wordsworth's time. Gaining an upper by-road, we saw Margaret and Dede in the distance, strolling towards us, both looking serene. Dede told me later that they had discussed mortality.

The pleasant scene remains in mind, assisted by the photographs we took.

When the time came to part, we drove our friends to Bath, and lunched with Charlotte in the Pump Room. Charlotte worked as deputy manager of the HMV branch in Bath.

Rain poured down that day. Gary and I took shelter in a tour of the Roman Baths while the ladies shopped. Our friends caught the London train from Bath station. Margaret and I drove back to Oxford, with Margaret again at the wheel.

We returned home late on Thursday. Wendy had been feeding our cats while we were away. For our part, we were happy to resume our prized and peaceful home life. But on the Saturday Margaret and I went to the Acland, where she was X-rayed.

Tuesday 29th July

Well, a dreadful day: I am apparently very unwell. I had a liver ultrasound scan at the Acland on Saturday, and the radiologist immediately told me I needed a biopsy, as there were 'irregularities', which ought to be investigated further. Neil phoned yesterday, Monday, to say it was rather worrying, as these growths could be evidence of a secondary CANCER. I can't remember whether he actually used that word, but that's certainly what he was talking about. But we have no evidence of a primary growth. He seems to think the heart condition might have disguised it. Although I had a colonoscopy which was totally clear two years ago, I may have a tumour there somewhere – though I never pass any blood. Christ! It's a death sentence. The encyclopedia says that once a secondary growth develops in the liver there's nothing that can be done.

B and I collapsed into each other's arms, wept and comforted each other, without really being able to believe it. Immediately, thoughts of all I want to put in order, of how desperate it would be to leave my darling husband to cope on his own, the children without seeing them

married and without seeing any of my very own
grandchildren . . . I have to stop myself brooding.

Having to stop herself brooding . . . Maybe. And having to commune within herself and summon up all her inner resources of fortitude.

Although we were to face much misery to come, it was always tempered by Margaret's wonderful example of courage and concern for others than herself.

On the following day, Sunday, she slept badly and spent much of the day simply lying about. Hardly suprisingly.

Tuesday 29th July

At 3.25 yesterday, Neil phoned to say there was a growth of secondaries on Margaret's liver, as revealed by her sonic scan on Saturday. Unwrapping this we found it meant cancer.

She will go to Mr Kettlewell for a liver biopsy on Wednesday.

We went into the living-room and held each other and wept.

My darling! – Why wasn't this me, with my checkered old life, instead of my dear young innocent wife?

O Rose, thou art sick!
The invisible worm
That flies in the night,
In the howling storm,
Has found out thy bed
Of crimson joy,
And his dark secret love
Does thy life destroy.
William Blake.

Now I entered a period of rapid mood swings, in contast with Margaret's amazing equilibrium, while we struggled to come to terms with this fatal news.

Being sensible and stalwart, my lady goes to Jo at Salon Scandinavia to have her hair done before tomorrow's biopsy.

This evening, she phones Tim in Brighton to issue a vague storm warning. 'It doesn't look too good,' she says brightly. Tim is concerned and says he will ring tomorrow. Today, she appears in good spirits but is clearly frail. She snoozes on my chaise-longue here in the study all morning long, and on the sofa in the afternoon. In part it must be the shock of the news.

Already it's started. 'This tree she planted with her own dear hands . . .'

Her gentle manners, her sweet and cheerful voice. I don't know what to do, where to turn. If only I could take on her cancer and she could live . . .

My vegetables have been a fair success this year, as I have fought weeds, pigeons, slugs, snails and blackfly on my little patch. It's hot and dry weather: I've just hosed everything down. The peas aren't brilliant, but the broad beans are delicious. Margaret ate some for her supper, in a white sauce.

Wednesday 30th July

We went to see Mr Kettlewell, a large, rugged, muttering sort of man in a loose grey suit. He sat in his room in Polsted House, next to the Acland, asking Moggins questions and examining her. There's to be no biopsy. We feel we've been given another week of life! After that week, a CT scan and then a laparoscopy. It appears there may be a tumour in the stomach or pancreas. I pray not the pancreas.

Margaret describes this anxious time.

I had a fairly immediate appointment with Mr Kettlewell, who has done my two colonoscopies; he took all the details, and sounded out my diaphragm; he found one uncomfortable patch between my ribs. He suggests a laparoscopy would be better than a biopsy, which is rather hit and miss: this would be a micro-camera put into the liver area so they can have a good look around it and other organs, pancreas, etc. Seems a good idea. In his mumbly quiet way, he was not nearly so fatalistic as Neil had been, and says there could be other reasons, and there is always chemotherapy (me!) and so on.

We came away feeling we had been granted a reprieve, and went into town to buy new photo albums etc. (I want to make Tim and Charlotte an album each of their family backgrounds – I have the photos chosen already).

Much of Margaret's character can be read in that extract. Her courage, her concern for others, her sense of family, her determination to act and get on with life.

On the day after the meeting with Mr Kettlewell, we both had health appointments. Mine I felt was completely irrelevant; it had been fixed some while earlier. Margaret describes it, not particularly flatteringly.

Yesterday morning early I had an appointment also with George Hart, my cardiologist, who also listened patiently to all the symptoms which have occurred since the angiogram last year. He took my blood pressure which he says is fine. No comment on my irregular, or rather increased, pulse rate. He says the laparoscopy is a good idea, and he will decide if I need to change medicines after the results of it come in. A cheery little fellow.

B had an appointment with an ENT consultant in the afternoon! We are making the most of our BUPA subs at present!! It was because of his permanently achy nose, dry and painful up the top. A very pleasant and clearly spoken youngish man (the sort Charlotte ought to get together with!) looked at everything and pronounced it normal, but said the septum dividing the nostrils was a little crooked, blocking one nostril slightly.

We talked of B's snoring, which I described as someone cutting corrugated cardboard with a serrated knife, which amused him; he suggests B might attend the sleep clinic locally, but that any operation to shave bits off the floppy palate is extremely painful and not recommended. There are other things that can be done.

B said to me he felt like a fraud, getting attention for his nose at present when it is a minor thing. Certainly while he is on Beconase and the two inhalers, his breathing is easier and he snores less.

But he is very tired, has bad legs, etc. and always has indigestion much like what I am experiencing at present, a cross between a hiccup and a burp. Mr Bates suggested losing a stone in weight would help B greatly, even with the snoring. We must try to aim for this – I'm sure it would help his legs too.

Last week at Tarr Steps, and driving up and down to Devon, I was pretty fit – but feel I couldn't manage it this week, that's pretty bad. Most mornings this week, I feel very shaky, pulse rate high, and not keen to stand still at all. I have just had to ask B to do the shopping. Poor man, he is looking after me extremely nicely and kindly and patiently, getting morning teas in bed, doing the washing up, clearing rubbish and putting out papers and bottles etc. Luckily he is not under too much pressure with work; White Mars *continues well, but does not have to be finished for quite a while; the autobiog. will need a lot of work, when Little, Brown agrees to release a marked copy of the mss. with suggestions.*

By this date, I had taken back my autobiography from HarperCollins and had changed publisher. I was now with Little, Brown.

For reasons that I now find hard to understand, I was somewhat astonished when Margaret asked me to *do the shopping*. I had become so used to her expeditions. Of course I trawled round Tesco's with her shopping list. Margaret never visited a supermarket again.

Margaret is to peck at a little food every hour. Chocolate was mentioned. This will suit her birdlike eating habits well. After Mr Kettlewell, we shopped in Summertown at the delicatessen, then called on Wendy and Thomas. I can see Moggins is a little scared of Thomas. He has become so boisterous, and rushes unpredictably at people in a boyish way. She is so delicate she fears he might charge into her.

With Thomas I played in their Victoria Road garden – dungeons and Exploding Boys. The dear ladies talked indoors, ever good friends. Wendy once paid Chris [Margaret] a great compliment, saying she wished she had been her mother. Certainly Margaret's mild behaviour, her kindness, her lack of stridency have made us all better people.

[II]

First week of August

Tomorrow, my darling first-born's thirtieth birthday; this time thirty years ago I was sitting in Jasmine garden with my feet up, very large, few cares in the world!

Now, who knows? This morning I am extremely shaky, even my writing is not what it was. Have I had this thing coming on for a long time? B looks back at his diaries and says I was unwell in the spring, but it was merely a sore throat I think.

The heart trouble has been with me for some time. But this new thing? I lie awake at night trying to sort out things in my mind, like what will happen to my belongings: my will is made, and is fine, but I've left nothing to Mark, or to Sarah [Sheridan, Tim's fiancée], or to Youla, which I'd like to do. Tim and Charlotte will get Quay House immediately, I suppose, and B will have to fund it for them while decisions are made about whether to keep the flat or not . . . Well, I can't look

after that for them, but it would at least give them some
funds to use for their own properties in due course.

My dearest step-daughter came up on Friday with a
wonderful large basket full of goodies and snacks for me!
Such thoughtful kindness as always. She and Mark are as
dear to me as my own two.

Charlotte called on Saturday, with some lovely flowers
for me. We talk, mostly superficially, about things. In the
car driving her back to her current boyfriend Owen's
place, I say there is a slight reason for worry about my
condition. She does not say much about that, perhaps
trying to be optimistic for my sake. We say we will see
each other in a fortnight.

Sarah has taken Tim over to France for twenty-four
hours for his big birthday, hiring a smart Rover 200 for
them – they hope to buy one next year! He sounded
extremely cheery on the phone!

It was difficult to see how much Charlotte understood
from her mother's lightly made remarks. Driving her into
town for her to meet up with Owen on another occasion, we
stopped outside Blackwells' art shop and had a fairly ghastly
conversation, where I had to tell her the omens were not
good. My hope was that she would prepare herself mentally
for graver shocks to come.

On the 2nd of August, we went to tea with our kind
neighbours, the Stantons, John and Helen. Also present were
Margaret and Jeremy Potter. Jeremy was slowly succumbing
to an inoperable cancer. He had tried chemotherapy, but it
made him feel so unwell he refused further treatment. He

seemed well enough at the table. But so did Margaret; she was bright and talkative. I could not believe she was under threat of death, so serene was her radiance.

Yet she grows weaker. Is it only my fancy she grows thinner and her eyes grow larger, mistier?

It's a long while to the 7th and the laparoscopy; the time till then seems like a gift we've been given yet cannot use.

Sunday 3rd August

If I had the effrontery to think of life as a spiritual journey, then Margaret is far ahead of me; so calm, so tender.

Clive phones from Athens to ask after her health. Although she tells him that one of her symptoms is rather worrying, she says it so reassuringly, so light-heartedly, with amusement even in her voice, as if to say *It's nothing*, that he and Youla are surely deceived into thinking all is well.

She's too tired to water the garden. I do it for her – and drench myself with the hose!

It was a wonderful sunny summer. In order to keep Margaret's thoughts directed towards the future, I was creating a new bed in the garden. It proved to be hard work.

Moggins sits and watches me plant honeysuckle to climb the new pyramid, and to set a new deutsia in the bed. Charlotte arrives, bringing flowers, for one of her lightning visits. We have tea and biscuits in the helix, and photograph each other.

Charlotte has presents for Tim's birthday.

Wendy calls at 8.30, large with child. She brings Chris a

basket of 'snack' gifts, knowing she can eat only a litle and often. A lovely and loving surprise! We're very cheerful.

It's been a nice day.

That night, I had a fragment of a dream, in which humanity had been given the gift of better understanding. I saw two people sitting together talking. A voice tells me, 'They are going over all the conversations they had in their lives, improving them.'

If only . . .

Somewhere in that long night, Margaret came to the realisation that our proposed holiday in Brittany would be too much for her. This was to have been a family holiday by the sea. She and Wendy had made all the arrangements between them. We had hoped for a repeat of a gorgeous holiday we had all enjoyed in Languedoc, in the heart of France, a couple of years earlier.

Brittany was not to be. Wendy and Mark also had their problems. Wendy was pregnant, with a demanding small boy at her heels, Mark was bowed with over-work, and they were going to move house.

Ordinary life continued in fits and starts. We drove to Yarnton Garden Centre and bought £72-worth of plants for the new bed as if nothing was wrong. Margaret walked happily among the assembled plants. Indeed, she was strong enough to bake us a delicious Bulgar plum pie for lunch – of which she could eat but little. She smiled sadly at me as I cleared away. Oh, my dear loving darling! Now you are gone, I live in the dull widower-world of hasty snacks, indifferent eating. I should have framed your lovely pie instead of eating it . . .

Food became an increasing problem for her. One of the concoctions in Wendy's magic basket of snacks was called 'Nurishment'. It was packaged in the average-size can and was manufactured by Dunn's River Nutritionals. 'Nurishment' became Margaret's stand-by. The drink was advertised as a meal replacement and an energy and nutrition boost. It came in several flavours, and contained vitamins, proteins, calcium and other necessaries. 'Nurishment' must have given Margaret at least an extra day of life – and much enjoyment.

Otherwise, she scarcely ate. I took her her breakfast in bed. She managed to eat half a piece of toast, spread with honey. As her appetite failed, so, empathetically, did mine.

Standing became a problem for her. We drove up to a big builders' showroom, Johnson's, and investigated stools or seats to use in the shower cubicle. I begin to ask myself guilty questions in the diary.

What can books, ornaments – work, indeed – mean if she is not here with me?

It was to be but a brief while before I found the answer to that question.

We extracted a note from Neil saying Moggins was unfit to travel abroad. I took it to Summertown Travel to cancel our Brittany holiday. There, a sympathetic lady named Karen set about retrieving some of our deposit through the insurers. As the transaction concluded, she said, 'Give my love to your wife.' It was so touching. I burst into tears on the way home, and had to draw the car into the side of the road. I still found it hard to accept what was coming to seem more and more inevitable. How Margaret managed, I cannot imagine. Perhaps her long sleeps helped.

But she slept badly that night. I took her some muesli to bed in the morning. It was all she asked for. She had no taste for tea any more, and drank mineral water, mainly Volvic, in the small bottles easily stored in the fridge. Soon after washing and dressing she looked as sparkling as ever and, as ever, made light of her ills.

How was our life then, poised on the brink?

I went shopping at the old Sainsbury's near Boars Hill. It was as quiet as a cathedral, with a few spectral oldsters wheeling their trolleys about in a funereal way.

Before lunch, I made the beds and vacuumed the bedroom. Moggins got some lunch together – Wendy's snacks, in part – after which we both had a nap. I worked on *Twinkling*. It's just a revision, easy to do, needing little real concentration. I'm earning nothing these days.

We drove into Oxford in the afternoon to buy some new toner for the photocopier. A brief outing. Clive and Youla rang during the evening, to see how Chris was.

Now 9.50 – dark and raining a little. Moggins is already in bed. I'm more or less watching the film version of Osborne's *The Entertainer*.

And tomorrow – O God! – it's the Acland!

She remains ever calm and sweet, reassuring others. A courageous lady!

If only we could have that day again, she and I! Even at the cost of having to watch *The Entertainer* once more . . .

So to the ghastly 7th August. I rose at 6.40, and prepared my poor sweetheart a modest breakfast of cereal. She did not clear her plate. We talked of our hopes and fears of what was to come that day, and clung to each other like shipwrecked sailors to rocks. We wept briny tears.

The Acland received us and a nurse conducted us to a small room labelled Room 3. It was hot and airless in there. I got a fan going. Margaret undressed and got into bed. There we waited, holding hands, silent now.

Eventually, an anaesthetist, the Chinese Mr Low, entered, talked informally, and took notes, detailing the heart condition. After him, nurses came, to prepare Margaret for the laparoscopy.

I suppose I left the hospital about three in the afternoon. As I went, the flowers I had ordered were delivered. I arranged them in a vase. Margaret was so calm; her dear smiles almost broke my heart. We hugged and kissed each other and I said I'd return at six, when she would be back in bed and recovering.

Our house was silent. The cats slept.

A laparoscopy is a serious matter. A slit is made near the navel and an endoscope inserted, by means of which the abdomen can be investigated. An endoscope takes the form of a fibreglass tube containing a lighting and lens system. A clawlike attachment can be inserted to cut a sample of tissue.

The worst news.

I was at the Acland before six, in plenty of time to see Moggins being delivered back into Room 3.

She was awake and on a drip, looking rather the worse for

wear. An analgesic suppository had been inserted into her anus. Beside the endoscope in her stomach, she had had a laryngoscope down her throat.

I sat by the bed and held her hand. We spoke a little. She asked after the cats. She was hot and I gave her some water.

It grew dark outside. Mr Kettlewell finally appeared. He muttered that the source of the secondary tumour on the liver had been traced to the pancreas.

It cannot be cured. Its progress might be slowed by chemotherapy, which treatment could be started almost at once. No wonder Kettlewell muttered. He had to deliver Margaret's death sentence.

She scarcely wept. This was everything we had feared. The all-devouring anaconda within . . .

A lady of massive kindness, by name Nikki Driscoll, an oncology clinical nurse specialist, then came in. She talked to us, explained, tried to reassure us.

She couldn't say how long my darling has.

Margaret had to remain in the Acland overnight. At last I had to drag myself away.

I returned to Hambleden. I have managed to speak by phone to all members of the family except Tim, who was working. Clive phoned almost as soon as I got home.

What Margaret's state of mind might be I cannot tell.

Farewell, our carefree happy days!

Friday 8th August

So, I brought her back from the Acland some time after noon. She was brave and bright. The Acland staff could hardly have been more considerate.

When we were home, she sat on the sofa. I made us
scrambled egg for lunch. Moggins followed it by yoghurt with
Greek honey. Then she slept for quite a while. Both Tim and
Charlotte phoned during the afternoon.

Margaret spoke a little about her bitter disappointment.
She had expected to enjoy another twenty years – time to see
Tim and Charlotte happily married, and producing
grandchildren. To grow old.

She was more unwell than she had been before entering
the Acland, and she suffered from the heatwave. I drove
to Currys superstore on the ring road and bought her a good
12-inch three-speed fan.

Moggins is upstairs now, having a cooling wash. Wendy is
coming to see her at six.

My dear Wendy! What an encouragement she was at this
time, despite her own troubles – of which she made light.
The babe within her had been diagnosed as having a slight
kidney problem, which would have to be rectified once it
(or *he*, rather, for we knew which sex it was by now) was
born. A report out at this time stated that 'the family is still
central to most people's lives'. In our case, it was stating the
obvious.

Saturday 9th August

Our practical, dependable Wendy arrived at six with a fine
standing fan for Chris! Unfortunately, I had pipped her at the
post; so she would use it in her own house. She also brought a
little bouquet of roses and a novel type of 'air cooler', which
we were to find very useful by Chris's bedside.

She stayed for an hour, while I watered the garden and prepared supper for my poor old battered girlie. She retired to bed after long phone conversations with Tim and Charlotte. They'll both be here next week, as will Clive, flying in from Athens.

When did this horrible thing begin to spread? As long ago as May of last year she could not face going to Israel with me. In September, in Portugal, she was rather under the weather. Yet in May this year, she seemed fine, although she had begun to leave her food. Clive took photographs of her on his balcony in Prigipou and she looks so well and beautiful, eyes bright, colour good. She's so brilliant in her own domain, so uncomplaining. Her heart trouble evidently masked this more insidious misery.

9.30. Her cheerfulness amazes me as much as her weakness troubles me. When did this weakness come on? So gradually we scarcely noticed . . .

During that last weekend in June, she seemed fine. Yet the next week, at Alex and Felicity's dinner, she could not eat, and fled the table to come home. I was worried then: why did I not rush her straight to Neil? But we assumed it was the heart, the pulse – to whose vagaries we had become accustomed.

And still I ponder the question – why were we not more suspicious? But we had a good GP in Neil MacLennan and a good heart specialist in Dr Hart, and neither of them raised the alarm until it was far too late. I lay no blame on them, although somehow one instinctively looks for someone to blame, if only oneself.

My diary entry for that sorrowful Saturday continues.

Today, after a misty start, has been calm, hot, serene. A lovely large bouquet of flowers arrived from Bet and Ant. I walked up to Hornby's the Pharmacist, to buy my wife some vitamins and face cream. Mrs Hornby not only knows her business but is sympathetic.

This afternoon I gardened, a euphemism for mucking out the filtration system that purifies the waterfall ... When the heat of the day had faded, I watered the flowerbeds. Margaret revived a little, and I persuaded her to sit with me in the shade of the house, where it was cool and we could hear the waterfall. We were together and content.

Idyllic though it sounds, my small engagement diary paints a more realistic scene that day. It simply says, 'Much crying . . .'

Margaret has no word in her log on this period of her decline. Not only had she to digest the reality of her situation, but the laparoscopy had greatly weakened her. We speculated about the possibility that the anaesthetic had damaged her heart, despite Dr Low's care.

There was also the heat.

Margaret was teaching me to cook, or at least to prepare the fish pies and other dishes I bought in the local supermarkets. Our tutorials were fun. But when the meals were presented to her, she had little appetite. I was forever buying too much food, and then having to throw it out, fearing it might have gone bad in the fridge.

The cats' milk went stale almost as soon as it was set down in its pottery bowl.

I was committed to buying the small plastic bottles of Volvic, always keeping at least two of them cooling in the fridge. She refreshed herself with this mineral water which, no doubt, her disordered liver required.

At one stage, a little later – but every week marked an epoch – I bought bottles of San Pelegrino, 'The Blessed San Pelegrino', as we used to call it when drinking it in Italy; but she had lost her taste for this particular water.

When did we first drink San Pelegrino? Perhaps it was one happy day when we had not been long married. We were in the Vale d'Aosta. In gloomy Aosta itself, we bought a chicken from a rotisserie, bread, a bottle of wine, fruit and a bottle of the sacred mineral water, and drove up into the mountains to eat. For our meal, we sat within sound of the Torrente Baltea Dora, plunging to destruction somewhere below.

The sky was dramatic, full of thunder and light. We toasted each other and drank the dark red wine and ate the chicken, while juice ran down our naked arms to our elbows. How happy were all our days then! That meal always remained in our minds, and the music of the Torrente Baltea Dora . . .

Sunday 10th August, and another heart-breakingly lovely day! But Margaret lies asleep in bed at 10.50, after taking pain-killers. 'I didn't expect the operation to set me back so much,' she said.

I did a little work on the new flowerbed before it became too hot. I grieve about the garden: her dear domain.

Our sweet Chagie arrived at about four, with prezzies for Mum. When she got here, I was upstairs helping poor M to be sick in the shower-room basin. I spoke to Charlotte first about the grave situation. She wept a little. However, both ladies recovered and spent a while quite cheerfully together.

Chagie says Owen has a Tamaguichi! No comment. Later, I
drove her back to his place in the wilds of Cowley. He provides
good support for her in a grave and challenging time.

Margaret now always lay quite late in bed, soothed by
Wendy's air cooler, trying to summon the energy to rise, wash
and dress. I began to help her climb slowly downstairs. At this
stage, we both expected her to recover from the laparoscopy,
and she had her plans for the future.

As to that future, we sat together often on our sofa, held
each other, and talked or read. We were both reading in
snatches Catherine Peters' *The King of Inventors*, the life of
Wilkie Collins.

Tim and Sarah had set their plans to get married in the
May of the following year. Margaret was determined to live
until then, even if it meant attending in a wheelchair. This
hope, or even expectation, buoyed us up. It did not seem
impossible at that time.

'And after the wedding,' I said, mock-seriously, 'you'll have
to hang on to see *Twinkling* published to great applause . . .'

On the following day, our doctor, Neil, came to see
Margaret. She had managed to get herself up after a slow
morning, during which I shopped at Budgen in
Summertown – one of the few places then stocking the
invaluable Nurishment.

Neil carries his own reassurance, but of course the cancer
is inoperable. He also brought reports on my problems, an
enlarged prostate and a cyst on my kidneys. I was less than
interested. He prescribed various drugs for Margaret to ease
her pains (her 'discomforts', as she called them).

Margaret kept her drugs in a neat little fabric case, and was punctilious in noting down what exactly they were. I have her latest card, although with various crossings out, due to changes in prescription, which happened frequently, it is now impossible to recall what she was being dosed with at any one time.

These pills include enalapril, dexamethasone, frusemide, co-proxamol (her standard pain-killer until near the end), potassium, flecainide and Luborant. Luborant was for her dry mouth. This group was to be taken at 9 a.m.

The 8p.m. group were, at various times, potassium, enalapril and flecainide, while at 9 p.m., in bed, she was to take HRT as usual, bendrofluazide and diazepam, the sleeping pill. Plus domperidone (not a brandy) when necessary.

The potassium was in liquid form. She found it disgusting, and ate bananas instead.

Neil mercifully cancelled Margaret's appointment for the lipid clinic. He stayed and talked for quite a while. Margaret was calm and not without humour.

My literary agent, Mike Shaw, returned from a holiday in the Canadian Rockies with his wife, Maureen, where Margaret and I had been eight years earlier. He reported on the offers Little, Brown was making for *Twinkling*, *The Squire Quartet* and *White Mars*. We both thought the offers were unreasonably modest, but I could summon little interest.

The hope of a literary reputation also has a cancer at its heart. I am not interested in anything, don't want to speak to anyone, outside the family. I just want to be solitary, to live with Margaret.

She read a great deal during her days, reserving a novel of Zola's for the winter, charmed by Lisa St Aubin de Teran's *A Slow Train to Milan*. Perhaps she was glad to be relieved of most household chores, although she never said so. We played music, Wagner's *Siegfried Idyll* being a favourite, taking on particular poignance now that our dear idyll, of such long-standing, was threatening to end. She listened frequently to BBC Radio 4 and, when she could, would return to her computer. Then, as we had done for so many unclouded years, we would both be sitting at our desks, working away, stopping for strolls round the garden, drinking coffee, talking, or perhaps reading.

We still had brief but anguished discussions of what was to come. As if her death was of minor significance, she often wanted to talk about what would happen to me. 'It doesn't matter,' I'd tell her. Nor did it. When she was in good form, I could not stop myself believing that she would somehow get better. Somehow.

On good advice, she had turned down the offer of chemotherapy. Neil, in his uninsistent way, was against it. Perhaps he knew the cancer was too far advanced (that was my thought, and it terrified me).

Tuesday 12th August

Tim rolled up in his DRU, a powerful Toyota off-roader he had bought and was repairing and refurbishing. He looked good, growing a beard and moustache, which suited him. He is staying overnight. (The rest of the world is asleep as I write.)

Moggins was so happy to see him. They embraced, she shed

a few tears. She was up and dressed, and had put washing in the washing machine (which she is belatedly teaching me to operate).

The heatwave still prevails, to her discomfort. My morning was spent shopping – still not my most brilliant act. To the vet for bag of catty 'Science Plan', and to Mrs Hornby for Neil's prescribed medicaments.

Then slowly into town, parking in the multi-storey. Long shop in M&S. Not only for food but for two No.16 cotton nighties. And tokens for Youla's birthday. Margaret was pleased with the nighties.

The three of us slept after lunch. Tim works so hard. He was very helpful, vacuuming with the Dyson, washing up, and later *mowing the lawn* while I fought the gruesome caterpillar attack on my purple sprouting brassica.

We were in quite good spirits, and ate supper by M's bed. I'm getting the hang of timing various things to be ready together, such as broad beans, new potatoes, and a haddock and asparagus pie.

Tim was thoroughly familiar with his mother's perilous situation. He had sensibly rung Neil and had everything explained to him.

As far as this tragedy can be explained. How can you believe that my lovely wife is going to die? To die!

Jesus. It's 2.15 on Wednesday morning. Silence prevails everywhere, smothers everything. What does she dream? Pray her dreams are full of light.

Every day seemed to us a day set apart. Margaret certainly retained all her critical faculties. I did not know she was writing her log, or leaving me careful instructions to make life easier after her death.

She was by no means a materialist, but she liked her rings and carefully listed them during this period. The list is a kind of poem to our years together.

	M's JEWELLERY 1984	Insurance values
1.	Wedding ring, 22 ct. gold, bought 1965	?
2.	Engagement ring, 18 ct. gold, 11-stone diamond cluster, diamond on each shoulder, bought 1965 from The Antiquary	£550
3.	Set of 8 ct. gold rings with agate or chrysoprase, by Wendy Ramshaw, given me by B (for Wendy, please)	£350
4.	Ring, rectangular amethyst in 18 ct. gold, bought by B in Brazil	£160
5.	Ring, 2 opals & 3 garnets in 9 ct. gold, bought by B	£95
6.	Ring, opal (chipped) set in diamond cluster in 18 ct. gold, inherited from Grandma Manson, given to Charlotte	£375
7.	Ring, 14 ct. gold, large opal in Art Nouveau setting, B bought for me at The Antiquary	£195
8.	Ring, small decorative gold band, inherited from Grandma Manson, given to Charlotte	£65
9.	Ring, small 'diamond/glass' flower, given to me by Nana Aldiss, and by me to Charlotte	£30
10.	Ring, 3 small sapphires & 2 small diamonds,	

*given to me by Dorothy Aldiss, and by me
to Wendy*   ?

11. *Ring, large turquoise in fancy silver setting,
     by Richard Roney-Dougle, B bought for me
     in Henley (for Sarah, please)*   £110

12. *Ring & matching pendant, Celtic design, B   £90 &
     bought for me*   £55

13. *Ring, pale amethyst in 9 ct. gold link
     setting, given me by Dorothy Aldiss*   £50

14. *Ring, 7 diamond half-hoop, in pretty 18 ct.
     gold setting, given me by Dorothy Aldiss*   £395

16. *Brooch, oval citrine set in pearls, given to
     me by Brian on Charlotte's birth*   £200

17. *Brooch, old cameo of Pallas Athene, gold,
     inherited from Grandma Manson (for
     Betty, please)*   £120

18. *Brooch, oval agate in gold setting, inherited
     from Grandma Manson*   £30

19. *Ring, 22 ct. gold, fancy double hoop, made
     by a Frenchman, which Brian bought for
     me in Dallas*   £250

20. *Brooch, old gold horseshoe set with one row
     half-pearls and one row corals, I bought in
     Oxfam for £5!*   £130

21. *Necklace, agate and cornelian stones, 38",
     gold linked with heart pendant, inherited
     from Grandma Manson, which I wore at
     our wedding*   £125

22. *Locket, old oval silver(?) on fancy silver chain,
     B bought for me in Oxfam*   £85

23. *Amber set, pendant, ring, earrings, in fancy
     silver mounts, which B gave me on Tim's
     birth (for Youla please)*   £145
24. *Ring, large oval amber, in fancy silver
     setting, bought in Poznan, Poland, with
     B's Polish royalties*   £75
25. *Ring, Danish, oval amber, in silver setting,
     bought in Denmark*   £60
26. *Ring, Danish, oval amber, in double silver
     setting, bought in Denmark*   £70
27. *Ring, Russian, oval amber, worthless*   –
28. *Ring, large grey smoky quartz, in very
     decorative silver mount, B bought for me*   £35
29. *Ring, yellow corundum in fancy gold(?)
     setting, B bought for me in Belgium*   £185
30. *Ring, pink rhodochrosite in 9 ct. gold
     decorative setting, B bought for me in Oxford*   £110
31. *Pendant, jadeite 'shark's tooth' set in 9 ct.
     gold, B bought for me in Singapore*   £120
32. *Bracelet, slim 9 ct. gold, inscribed MM, B's
     first present*   £30
33. *Bracelet, solid gold, heavy links, swivel clasp,
     B bought for me in Nieman Marcus, Dallas
     (for Wendy please)*   £3,250

In the study, we had acquired two new box files, and with their aid all the filing was reorganised, so that income and expenses filtered straight into the boxes, instead of accumulating in the wire in-tray as formerly. The rest of the correspondence, papers of all kinds, was filed at once in the filing cabinet.

So to another day, another day of intense heat. I feared the food was going off as soon as bought. Flies buzzed into the kitchen because the cats would not finish up their Felix.

Wednesday 13th August

Tim was very good and his visit greatly pleased his dear mum (and me!). Sarah sent Moggins a sweet note.

I made Tim and me a salami and lettuce sandwich before he set off back to work in Brighton. Sad to see his chunky DRU pull out of the drive gateway . . .

Moggins was up and dressed in a light summer dress some while before that. She sat on the sofa and rested, and stayed in the study for a while, keen to communicate with Dede. Dede and Gary have been great, keeping in touch by e-mail.

After some gentle persuasion, I went round next door to the Stantons to tell them of the fatal diagnosis. John and Helen were extremely sympathetic.

'No denying it's grim,' said John. Being a member of the cloth, he will add Margaret's name to his private prayer list. I stayed half an hour and was comfortable with them. We're fortunate to have such neighbours.

I grew a marrow, took great care of that marrow, and today I cut it and prepared it, stuffing it with pork sausage meat. Margaret sat by on her orange stool and advised me. We couldn't help laughing. I anointed the baby, wrapped it in foil and shoved it in the oven.

Later, we tried a tiny slice of it. Tough is what that marrow was!

She was in pain, and it was not time for another co-proxamol. So she took herself off to bed.

Meanwhile, Clive and Youla had arrived at Wendy's. I drove over there for an hour or so. I feel bad about not having them here in our spare room, as on previous occasions, but it's more than I can cope with. Besides which, I need an hour of solitude in the evening before going up to join Moggins. I drink a little San Pelegrino and eat a single square of Ritter chocolate. This is my apotropaic ritual.

Anyhow, Clive and Youla seemed none the worse for their flight. They all ate a takeaway, sitting in the garden as dusk fell. It was life as normal, except for Chris's absence. All were cheerful. Hard not to be with Thomas there.

Dear old family!

If I lay some emphasis on our family, it is in part because the unity and community of it was so fortifying. My early family life had been impossibly difficult, as I relate in *Twinkling*, while Margaret had always regretted her solitary childhood as an only child.

In the evening I wrote poems to try to come to terms with what was happening to my wife. Here is one of the first.

Rest Your Weary Head Upon Your Pillow

Rest your weary head upon your pillow,
Try to regain some ease.
While you're within my care I'll serve and love you
And lift the glass of water to those lips
I kissed so passionately long ago.
Let me suffer with your suffering, please,
And die with you each day as living slips

Further into the chill zone of co-proxamol,
Bendrofluazide, and domperidone.

Rest your weary head upon your pillow.
Try to regain some strength.
I'm with you and will wash and iron your garments
And smile back to that gently smiling face
I read with all concern. Minutes and seasons
Slip away – and each of lesser length;
Curtains more drawn, footfalls more soft to place.
'Are you awake, love?' Bless the hours when she
However faintly gives the answer, Yes . . .

Not only did I write a poem. I also rang our builder, Roger
Carter, asking him to rip out our shower cabinet, which was
about the size of a sentry box, and to install a better one, with
a tip-up seat in it on which Margaret could sit while washing
herself.

Thursday 14th August

Another hot, still summer's day. Weather lying in wait for
something awful to happen?

I dreamed I was staying in a hotel where the amiable female
proprietor had found a way of making permanent things from
that ephemeral stuff, newspaper: her banisters, for instance.

I seemed at one point to pick up the knack from her, and
was preparing to make a suitcase from a broadsheet paper.

But a distraction arose. A group of high-spirited young
guests decided to walk to a place called – was it Schraeding? I
went with them across the lawn to a road, where we were to

turn left (some indecision regarding this) – but I decided to take the road straight ahead, and to go on alone.

It was a long road. The sky was bright with sunset ahead; the sun, being obscured, lit the thin cloud with gold. This was a conscious echo of my recurrent life-dream, which first visited me at the age of five and returned in time of crisis. I have written of it elsewhere.

I came not to a church but a temple. The emphasis was Eastern. Entering without hesitation, I found a yellow and decorated room. In a recess, a man in a gold silken gown was at prayer; his back was turned to me.

A curious element of the dream was this: that while on the road I could distinctly hear hymn-singing from a church.

> *Fast falls the eventide.*
> *The darkness gathers,*
> *Lord, with me abide.*

A comforting dream. Inwardly, I was coming to terms with our situation. I roused. Margaret lay beside me, already awake and in some discomfort.

I got up, went downstairs, and brewed her a mug of Earl Grey tea, without milk.

I wondered what dreams she was having, but she never told me.

(All this is being written in the cool premises of the Oxford Volvo HQ. I'm sitting out an hour of a MOT service on H763 DFC. Our year's licence has already run out.)

Clive and Youla will visit No. 39 at 11 a.m. I hope to get back by then.

8.30 p.m. Margaret in bed after a poor supper. She still seems to have bruising in her stomach, resulting from the laparoscopy [This assumption was incorrect, I believe; the cancer was spreading, and causing her pain.]

I did some gardening, put more plants in new bed, and watered. Then washed up.

Margaret has now settled for the night. A good moon shines in at her window. Half an hour's quiet and a read of Freeman Dyson before I go up. Pelegrino, Ritter. Jones tomorrow. A crumb of hope there.

Friday 15th August

Up early, got Margaret a scrap of breakfast. Had a little cuddle. She looked pale, but seemed somewhat better than yesterday. As ever, she behaves very brightly – and looks good in one of her new nighties.

I got to Tesco's smartly at 9 a.m., pushing my trolley about there for an hour before going to hunt for a stool on which Moggins might sit while in the shower. No luck so far.

We're seeing and hearing a lot about celebrations in India (and Pakistan to a lesser extent) regarding fifty years of independence from Britain. One feels quite sentimental about it.

Mike Shaw rang. He had upped Little, Brown's offer on the books. I told him about Margaret's illness. 'Fucking awful,' we both agreed.

After a bite of lunch, she and I slept, then went out into the glorious day and drove to see Dr A.C. Jones in the oncology ward of the Churchill Hospital – just a stone's thrown from where she gave birth to our dear old kiddies, Tim and Chagie.

Jones was brisk and pulled no punches. Chemotherapy might or might not work. We should think about it.

He gave her . . . well, only months, at best.

The poor brave lady did then shed a tear. A ghastly shock.

Messengers bearing bad news are traditionally unpopular. I took against efficient Dr Jones in his new brown shoes.

Margaret of course was more charitable.

So we went to oncology dept. and had a session with one Dr Jones. He gave us the facts, straight. I only have months left. Let's hope it is double figures. He described chemotherapy, but said only a one in three chance that it would help, and at that probably not very much; also it might give me heart pains. Brian was there. We both wept.

He gave me steroids and female hormones.

Saturday 16th August

Sunny day. Nice Sue Brack (a neighbour of whom Margaret was very fond) rings. Margaret's in bed, looking bright. Sue has a leaky heart valve. Margaret describes her terminal illness to Sue as 'just one of those things . . .'

I can't believe it!

I gently chide her later, saying that for me there were only two events ever, the creation of the universe and her illness.

Margaret laughs. 'I don't expect other people to see it quite like that.'

She *gives the appearance* of taking this disaster lightly. Of course, her sensibilities differ from mine, in that she has them.

I wrote and broke the news to Joan and Harry Harrison. We know they'll be upset. How long have we known them?

The steroids seem to have a beneficial effect. Moggins is more lively today – rose and took a bath mid-morning. Slept heavily on the sofa after a little lunch, but ate a Marmite sandwich with the crusts removed and drank a glass of milk for her tea.

Her complexion is more sallow. She has lost another half-stone. Now she potters, watering the indoor plants.

She has almost decided not to undergo chemotherapy.

This decision tormented me. It was not that I questioned it; I just felt that it was unlike her not to fight adversity, and chemotherapy seemed like a last defence. Dr Jones put her off the idea of attacking this deadly thing, warning her that it might bring on chest pains. It was quite a barrage, to my mind: although later we did not find a doctor who disagreed with him.

Sunday 17th August

She rose quite soon after breakfast, showered, shampooed and came downstairs looking elegant, and seemingly without a care in the world. I can hardly believe it. Charlotte arrived at 8.30 last evening, so of course that's a source of cheer. She's been brilliant this morning, vacuuming, etc., and preparing for a family get-together about noon.

This party was not my idea. I had wondered about its wisdom. But Margaret had discovered a new lease of life from somewhere, to preside happily over the gathering.

Brian's birthday 18th August

Time has come and gone. The laparoscopy I had on the 7th really knocked me back quite a bit, left me very dopey and lacking totally in energy. Kettlewell gave us the bad news that it was definitely tumours in liver as well as pancreas. He suggested I have an interview with the chemotherapy dept. at the Churchill, meanwhile dished out pain-killers and minerals, etc. Very nice staff there, he's decent, and I was visited by the oncology nurses, particularly Nickie, who was sweetness and kindness itself.

The steroids bucked me up so much next day that I was out watering flowerbeds with the hose, walked as far as B's new bed, and stayed up later in the evening; also ate quite well. Previously being sustained by Nurishment which Wendy found, good milk shake containing minerals and vitamins.

Today the steroids have bucked me up so much that I wake at five, cannot sleep again, and do not sleep after lunch for the unconscious-type doze I have been having.

Yesterday, the whole entire dear family came up here to celebrate Brian's birthday, also a late celebration for Tim's thirtieth. They brought prepared dishes. Tim fished out our barbecue, Sarah and he did lamb kebabs, veggie kebabs, Wendy and Youla did salads, dips and scrummy puddings, lime & mascarpone pie and strawberry shortcake. A real feast, late but delicious!

Then B and I had a doze (or not) while the others made themselves scarce. We gathered again for tea and a delicious strawberry mousseline cake I had ordered *and Wendy had collected from Patisserie Pascale in Summertown. B opened some presents, very successful in particular was the garden kneeler from Tim and Sarah!*

Thomas in good form, but demanding and 'a cheeky monkey' as B puts it. I gave him the new sweater I recently knitted . . .

By 6.30 I was flagging, so they all washed up, tidied up, left us some goodies, and departed. Charlotte & Owen went to the pub with Tim & Sarah, to have a chat.

My wonderful children have turned out to be competent caring adults, and I am thrilled; Charlotte stayed the night with us, which was lovely, and leaped up Sunday morning to hoover and clean, as Tim had done the week before.

They were all determined to make us happy. In which enterprise they greatly succeeded – not least because Moggins with her smart new earrings looked gorgeous, sitting out in the helix with us and seemingly well.

How super and sweet everyone was! We had a game of tag, and played about like kids, while Moggins sat and filmed us on Mark's camcorder. Playing the cassette now, one can hear her pleasant laughter, entirely involved in the caprices of the game. It was particularly good to talk to Mark about Chris's condition. It was hard to realise how ill she was on this occasion.

Sarah was charming and affectionate; Tim's lucky there. We only wish Chagie was as fortunate. Owen had a hangover and was almost mute throughout the proceedings. That's what, in the army, we used to call a self-inflicted wound. Still, it was good-hearted of him to come at all . . .

While we sat at table, Thomas helped me unwrap my presents. I received:

. . . a Teas Maid from Moggins. I roared with laughter when I opened the parcel and saw what it was. It seemed so utterly middle class and old-fashioned! I exclaimed on what old crocks we had become. She laughed too.

I could not help remarking on how different it was from our days of roughing it in Jugland, as we always called the former Jugoslavia. She was philosophical. 'Well, we've done some exciting things, and on the whole we've been healthy.'

Her philosophical attitude amazes me. She seems less distressed than I am.

A very affectionate and kind message came by fax from Joan and Harry. We've know each other as a foursome for so long.

After tea, I drove to North Oxford and dropped a third draft of *White Mars* in on Laurence Lustgarten. Laurence is kindly drawing up a constitution for Mars. Went to call on Anthony and Catherine Storr in Chalfont Road. I had to tell them of Margaret's misfortune. We went into their garden and conversed while drinking some of Anthony's S.E. Australian Shiraz. Very fruity. It was a beautiful evening, and I was with a couple I much admire. I even felt happy most of the time I was there.

Returning home, I found Margaret turning out drawers. She's stronger, thank God, pro tem. We phoned Jeremy Potter to see how he was getting on, and watched episode twelve of *Jewel in the Crown* on TV.

On many occasions I had to announce to someone that Margaret was terminally ill. It was an alarming thing to have to do. Some were so shocked. Some women cried. Some did not know what to say, and were embarassed. A friend phoned from California and spent ten minutes telling me he did not know what to say. I did not care much for this; in such circumstances, it was a sign of egotism to concentrate on one's own feelings.

Much to be preferred was the response of Angela Burdick, an Oxford writer I did not know particularly well, who, when I told her, just seized me and hugged me. She understood instinctively that this was a case for something more than words.

Perhaps women are better at expressing their feelings than men – but then this was because of my own male attitude. Actually, I admired the response from the bursar of my old school, West Buckland, who was the commander retired of the Bermuda dockyard. 'Chin up, Brian!' he said.

Yes, well, damned sound advice.

But a bit difficult to maintain on all watches.

Of course, words have force. Certain words, coupled with another, acquire mysterious power – 'Nazi gold', for instance. 'Wife's death' is another. However one hedged this concept about, one was always aware of its shocking effect on the psyche of those whom one had to tell. There was another reason, less honourable, why making this awful announcement made me uncomfortable.

I could not help recalling a passage from *David Copperfield* in which Charles Dickens shows his understanding of human psychology.

Copperfield is at school when Mrs Creakle gently breaks the news to him that his mother is dead.

> If ever a child were stricken with sincere grief, I was. But I remember that this importance was a kind of satisfaction to me, when I walked in the playground that afternoon while the boys were in school. When I saw them glancing at me out of the windows, as they went up to their classes, I felt distinguished, and looked more melancholy, and walked slower. When school was over, and they came out and spoke to me, I felt it rather good in myself not to be proud to any of them, and to take exactly the same notice of them all, as before.

The recollection made me uncomfortable. One element certainly did give me satisfaction: that, following Margaret's example, I could speak of her forthcoming death without a tear in my eye, a tremor in my voice.

My fears and sorrows were greatly for her. But I was aware that the time would come when I would be thrown into the solitudes much like those I had experienced before I had had the good luck of meeting her. Although there were undoubtedly many couples facing much the same tragedy as we, the sorrowful drama of our particular case set us apart. Well, to be honest, not entirely apart, since all the members of the family were, to say the least, disconsolate; but they were young and had their young lives they must lead.

The chemotherapy question still hovered. Shortly after my birthday, Margaret made a final decision.

Today I talk to Neil MacLennan on the phone and discuss chemotherapy, which I am reluctant to have; I want my poor old body to be left in peace. He seemed to agree that that was wise; B thinks we might need more information on chemotherapy and try it out. Neil phoned the Michael Sobell House (it has come to be time to mention this hospice, the final caring place for many people), and spoke to the head of it, who also felt it was sensible not to have chemotherapy.

I have lost a stone in weight, and it shows. But I am happy here with my darling Brian, who is coping with all his new chores most wonderfully.

We ring some domestic agencies to get some cleaning help. Mrs Wilkinson has retired, otherwise I feel out of the goodness of her heart she might have come up here. She is going to have a cup of tea with me anyway this week.

So many kind friends sending good wishes. Such loving e-mails from Harry Harrison, who finds it so difficult to express emotion, but it comes over. I reply saying fancy it being me of the four of us to go first . . .

Had she really adjusted in this remarkably calm way? I felt it necessary to hide my own wild despair from her. Her path was stony enough without her having me flinging myself about and worrying her about how I would be.

It's only in my notebook that I ask, in large letters,

HOW
CAN I POSSIBLY
LIVE
WITHOUT HER?

We wake in the night and are calm. We're in each other's company. We walk through into the airy book-room where, in this heat, the double windows stand open all night. I clutch her cool candy arm, breathe her sweet scents. She's with me: surely she's well. *Surely* she can't die.

But what does she think about it?

Tuesday 19th August

I heard Margaret say over the phone today – perhaps to Ulla – 'I am in good spirits.' It's true. So she is.

The fine weather and early dawns tempt one to rise. I was up at 6.15 and working on the day, since our favourite builder, Roger Carter, was due at 9a.m. to measure up for a new improved shower, with a seat for Margaret.

Busy morning. M up quite promptly, looking scrummy. Made a lunch of fried egg, baked beans and toast, which she enjoyed. Then we rested and slept.

I walked up to Somerfields supermarket and shopped. Once I dreaded the place; now it's home from home. Kindly motherly lady cashiers.

Liz Spink [our chiropodist] came and was shocked by Margaret's news. Liz is good news – what my parents called 'a cure'.

Liz called on me in December, after Margaret's death, and told me that Margaret had said she worried about me, since

I was growing old and needed looking after; she said nothing about herself.

Later, Tim and Sarah came with her parents, Clive (known for convenience as Big Clive) and Rosemary. We chatted for a pleasant half-hour. Sarah's car has broken down in Wantage. I drove them to Eurocar, to rent a Ka. Back to pick broad beans and prepare supper. Watered garden. God, what a boring account.

I was somewhat running myself into the ground, writing hastily when Margaret had retired to bed. She was always quite eager to go and read more of the work of Lisa St Aubin, etc. Her Argentinian episode greatly fascinated Margaret. We had become quite involved with this lady's life on paper. I had met her at a Cape party when she was married to a friend of mine, the gloriously eccentric George Macbeth.

Margaret's kind weaving friend Scilla called and presented her with a lovely bouquet of flowers. It stands here in our hearth.

Tim's very good and reliable. I can discuss things with him. He shows his concern in practical ways – for instance, by mowing the lawns in the heat.

My friend Scilla from weaving turned up with a superb bouquet of flowers, didn't stop, but hopes I will visit her next week. I hope so too. Other friends seem to be too nervous to write, send cards, or flowers . . .

I am very shaky in the mornings, my best time seems to be from 3–8.00 p.m.!

*B so tired, especially with this dreadful humid heat,
most peculiar for this country – it may reach the
unrecorded figure of 100 degrees before it breaks.*

*The next day we went to Sobell House to talk to Dr
Twycross. Such a very pleasant good-humoured chap,
about our age, seeming to have endless time for us; asked
all the questions about symptoms & pills, etc., and what
had I come to him for. Slightly flummoxed, I
remembered it was supposed to be about whether to have
chemotherapy. Definitely no, he said, he would not even
recommend it for his wife in the same state. Nothing
much to be done then, except maintain the quality of life
as well as possible. Such a kind and loving Macmillan
nurse with him, Patti Pugh, who hugged me as we
walked along the corridor – exactly what one needs,
physical comfort. She and or a colleague will call on us
here. At present I am so hot and cold together, my heart
races if I move around a room, and I have to sit down
and breathe fast. Pretty useless really! I can perch on the
high stool and wash up, sit and put things in the oven or
washing machine, but no hope of Dysoning or
dusting . . .*

*We ring a cleaning firm and book them to come and
do us over once a week.*

*Sue Brack has promised to send her gardener round to
see us and discuss helping.*

*Brian does all the shopping and catering, mostly we
live on delicious fish pies and fresh green beans from
the garden. Poor B does so much for me, always
running round.*

I enjoyed it. It was my way of shedding that stone in weight, as recommended by Mr Bates, the ENT man.

In fact I was learning, under Margaret's tutelage, to do many things I should have learned to do years earlier, such as cooking simple meals and understanding the codes on the washing machine.

Margaret was now receiving visitors in the afternoon. One afternoon, along came our friend Joyce Wilkinson, looking very bonny. She stopped and talked with Margaret for two hours. She and husband Pete were planning to fly to New Zealand, now that he was so much better after a triple heart bypass. Too bad the pancreas bypass has not yet been invented.

We had often been advised to enjoy ourselves while we could. A long ocean cruise was suggested, a flight round the world. We thought these were events one was sentenced to. Our great pleasure was to remain in peace and quiet at home together, enjoying each day as it came – with the occasional foray abroad.

Now that Margaret was feeling slightly better, our plans revived to go Eurostar to Paris. We had always intended to travel through that splendid engineering achievement the Channel Tunnel, and had tried to book on the first train to go through; but at that time there was no booking system and, with all the delays to traffic, the opportunity passed. Margaret also wished to see her flat in Blakeney again, as well as going back to Scotland to walk in – or at least gaze upon – the Ochils, which she had known as a wee lass, and in which she and I had walked in the days before we were married.

For a short while, this seemed a modest and realisable ambition.

Wednesday 20th August

Margaret has had breakfast and is bathing. It's not so hot today. She is enjoying sorting out her belongings, her jewellery and so forth, deciding who shall have various rings, etc.

She has decided to buy me a Volvo 850! – Another birthday present.

Her kindness shows itself in the way she tries to protect me from the demon housework. Feeling in better fettle, she hung out the washing, and washed up some dishes, perched elegantly on her orange stool.

Hard to recall that it is only four weeks ago that we had that halcyon break on Exmoor with Dede and Gary. All seemed well then. Alas, alas! My poor darling girl!

Then the following day:

Rising early, I drove to Johnson's to buy tiles for the improved shower. It's a modest improvement, for which Carters' will charge me a grand and over.

At 12.30, M and I set out for Sobell House, in the grounds of the Churchill Hospital where, I suppose, my dear lady will end her days.

There was nothing untoward in her manner; it might have been just a casual visit to see a friend.

The Sir Michael Sobell House, to give it its proper name, is Oxford's celebrated hospice. It was established twenty years ago, bearing the name of the President of the National Society for Cancer Relief, who donated a generous capital sum to the Oxfordshire Health Authority, if that authority would cover the running costs.

Hospices once seemed a revolutionary idea. But as medicine became more and more concerned with curative treatment and high technology, those for whom nothing more could be done were increasingly sentenced to second-class care. Doctors preferred beds to be taken by more 'interesting' patients.

The hospice makes no attempt uselessly to cure. Thus they obey Arthur Hugh Clough's satirical *Second Decalogue*:

> Thou shalt not kill; but need not strive
> Officiously to keep alive.

The patients of a hospice are tended and permitted a dignified end.

Whatever Margaret felt, and undoubtedly she sensed a need for the place, I experienced no eagerness to enter its glass portals. Within a short time, I was to come to cherish the refuge and rely on it for some support myself. As an anniversary book published by the house claims, 'Those visiting it for the first time often comment that it is not the gloomy and depressing place they had imagined it to be. Instead they find a place which is full of life and even joy. A strange discovery indeed! Life and joy in the midst of death and distress. But it is perhaps in this paradox that the "secret" of Sobell House resides.'

Entering the doors of Sobell, you turn left for the patients' department or right for the staff offices. We walked along the right-hand passage, escorted by a nurse, to the office of Dr Twycross, a gentle and understanding man. The Macmillan nurse sat almost silent as we talked. At first I wondered why she was present, but I came to understand that she was taking mental note, not only of Margaret's case, but of her personality. Patti Pugh proved to be good news for us.

She won me over when, as Margaret says in her log, she put her arm about her as we walked away down the long corridor. We were to see more of her as the cancer progressed.

Macmillan nurses are special people, trained for hospice work, which entails working closely with GPs and district nurses. They can advise patients and their families, not only in the hospice but in the home. In other words, they fill a space which was previously a vacuum. I grew fond of Patti, who had a good sense of humour, and was fearless but far from unfeeling in facing the acute grief that suffering and death bring to all involved.

It seems that a Macmillan nurse's salary is paid in part by the NHS and in part by private donations. Sobell House is itself run in this peculiarly English way. It seems to work.

Gary and Dede were particularly interested in this system, and said they wished there was such a system in America. Certainly there is a hospice system in the States but I gather it is privately run.

Funding Sobell House must present difficulties, but one advantage of the dual funding system (in other respects by no means ideal, one would guess) is that reliance is placed on volunteer labour. Not all the orderlies, receptionists, and others are professionals. Among them are men and women who have reason to be grateful to Sobell, or have found their loneliness assuaged by the team work involved. It really is 'a place full of life' as the brochure says – yet a place where you go to die.

So, what happened during our visit?

We were taken to Dr Twycross, a large, kindly and considerate man, possibly a golfer, who asked questions and listened intently to Margaret's answers.

He's against chemotherapy too, so that settles it. You have to believe what such a man says. If he were Russian he could hardly be more impressive. We do nothing: wait for the end and make the best of things. There's no hope. M was mainly dry-eyed, but wept a little. I clutched her hand, gave her a handkerchief.

Andy Durban [our financial adviser] sent Margaret a splendid basket/bouquet of flowers.

Anthony and Catherine came to tea and wine. All very pleasant amid a lot of laughter – although, as with Mrs Wilkinson yesterday, the visit was slightly too long for my poor Moggins. Now 9.15, she's in bed resting.

What the day entailed for her and her emotional resources is impossible to say. Was then, is now, for ever more shall be.

Friday 22nd August

She seemed rather faint today. I ascribed it to the sheer negativity of the news yesterday. However kindly put, it permitted no hope. How could anyone withstand that?

Could it be that she has only a few more – not years or months, but *weeks* left? The idea strikes a chill into my heart. Oh, oh God, if only I might die with her . . .

Wendy drove over with Thomas, bringing with her Clive and Youla. I've seen so little of Clive. It bothers me. They brought more Nurishment. It was difficult to talk with Thomas constantly doing his attention-grabbing act. I saw how frayed Moggins was getting and had to drop a hint.

And shortly after they arrived, along too came Jane Rugoyska, with her photographer, to reconnoitre the garden for next Friday's shoot. She is doing a programme on insomnia for Anglia TV. I need this like a hole in the head, but the process started long ago – almost in Heath House, you might say, when I contributed to Hilary Rubinstein's anthology *The Complete Insomniac*. I believe I was the only man he could find who actually liked insomnia. Insomnia provided a creative time, as long as you went outside into the night. Jane had picked up my article. I liked Jane, so I went through with the filming, despite its inconvenience to all here. I introduced Clive to her.

For lunch M and I had a quarter each of a Spanish melon. Moggins also ate a Marmite sandwich, sans crusts as usual, I, paté on toast. Yoghurt.

Afternoon sleep.

I decide to treat Brian to a new(ish) Volvo 850! Well, it is really my birthday present to him! He has been longing for one for ages! (So have I!)

We drive down to Motorworld, I sit in the car while B chats to a pleasant young salesman; he looks over a nice turquoise model, P reg., 8,000 miles only, and decides that is the one!! We get quite a good deal, we think. I walk round it – it is still extremely hot weather, so too hot to get into, but it's really smooth: climate-controlled! We hoped we could swop cars then and there, but of course it can't be done until next week, so we come home patiently, gloating! The interior is so identical to our present one

that all the switches should be in the usual place for B,
and he will be able to go on driving it for some years.
Whether or not I will do much driving remains to be seen.
Shall we ever get to Blakeney again? All those stairs . . . So
many visitors at present, somewhat exhausting!

Why did she decide to buy me that car? Perhaps on reflection she considered the Teas Maid had not been a total success; it sat in a corner of the bedroom, unused, because I needed to get up when I woke, for the sake of my legs: so it was healthier to go downstairs and make us mugs of fresh tea.

Whatever her motives, she must have wanted to do it for the pleasure of pleasing me; and she was looking ahead, as usual, because our H reg. Volvo 720, with 80,000 on the clock was, frankly, inching towards the banger class.

And she knows I'd never buy a new car on my own.

Whatever her reasoning behind the gift, it was all done charmingly, even playfully. I was delighted.

The garage allowed us £4,500 on the old model. We collect the new car on Tuesday.

She seemed pretty well today, despite the long-continuing heat. She constantly uses her Spanish fan.

[III]

A short passage in the *Upanishads* took me a while to understand:

> There are two birds, two sweet friends, who dwell on
> the self-same tree. The one eats the fruits thereof, and
> the other looks on in silence.
>   The first is the human soul who, resting on that
> tree, though active, feels sad in his unwisdom.

For some while, I had seen these two birds in myself. There was always a part of me which looked on detachedly at the folly and ambition and general unwisdom of the other more active part.

Now I perceived myself as the one bird and Margaret as the other, the observer, in our union, our little fruit tree. Was not hers a great wisdom – one I could not myself attain – in refusing to grieve over her oncoming death, but to accept that it was a part of her existence?

Regarding that matter, there is another passage in that same ancient Eastern book that strikes home:

> It is not for the love of a wife that a wife is dear; but
> for the love of the Soul in the wife that a wife is dear.

Certainly that was the present case. I loved the soul, that irreplaceable soul, I perceived in her, in these days of her suffering.

Saturday 23rd August

Waking at six, I got up while Margaret slept, and did some work. It was light and pleasant; the morning invited me.

Moggins sweats a good deal. I wish they would get a move on with the shower. She bathed, washed her hair, dressed. She is helpful when she can manage it, washing up, peeling runner beans, watering nearby plants – all performed sitting down. When she can manage it. She is very weak and pants almost continuously.

Yet when I see her doing normal tasks, my hopes betray me into thinking, Oh, she can't die, she can't! It's a lie, an illusion!

I shopped in the local Somerfield. I can walk there and back. It's begun to feel like home. I'm cordial with the cashout ladies, those prisoners of commerce.

When I returned, letting myself in the side gate, there she sat at her computer as in days of old, waving cheerfully. And again I hope. My love, stay there for ever, even if you're a little unwell.

When I go and give her a kiss, I see she is typing e-mails to her friend Lucia Elpi, another cancer sufferer, in Bologna, and to the Storrs.

My friend Andy Richards drove in and bought some books from me. I helped him carry them downstairs and stow them in his car. He will pay cash in ten days. I trust Andy. He's a good pal.

At 5.15 came our other visitors – Viscount David Samuel, his wife Eva, and another academic, by name also David. David Samuel, with whom I had been in correspondence, is a chunkily handsome man, clearly still very lively and active.

These Davids were of intense interest. Both had been in India and Burma during the war, and were actually on the Mandalay campaign. Samuel had then gone on to Sumatra – indeed, at one time had been virtually in charge of it – 'had the keys of it', as he said. He was then a major whereas I was a mere signalman, but we had taken the same exotic path, all those years ago. He was even in 26 Indian Division, the 'Tiger Div', as I was.

Under David Samuel, the Dutch who had been incarcerated in Japanese prison camps were allocated berths on the locally famous ship, the S.S. *Van Heutz*.

He says the Jap army had no wish to surrender. There were five thousand of them, as against five hundred British. A compromise had to be arrived at, whereby the Japs were allowed to retain their weapons, and were consulted every morning. On more than one occasion, they fought with the British against Indonesian forces. It was a strange situation, hardly recorded in the history books.

What a fantastic time that was! And how enjoyable, really! The excitement of it, the moments of joy, the danger!

We had a wonderful afternoon's conversation; which could scarcely have interested Margaret as much as it absorbed the Davids and me.

She went to bed that night at 8.30. Then I was sorry that, during that long conversation, I had neglected her.

Oh my sweetest darling, I can't yet believe the time will come – all too soon! – when your name will be something I can but cry in an empty house. I love you so, so dearly! With you gone – oh, my love, what can there be left for me?

Now I am in the unenviable position of being able to answer my own rhetorical question: there can be this book. The moment that has provoked it was then still to come.

Sunday 24th August

Always now, dreams of loss. What can Moggins's dreams be like? Are they luminous? She doesn't tell. Last night I dreamed she left in a car, and was going to be away for a while – for a *while*! – without kissing me good-bye. I walked in a wood deep in dead leaves.

I woke before six, rose, came down, disconsolate, to the study, worked on bloody *Twinkling*, while she slept her poor weary sleep upstairs.

It proved to be a peaceful day. With apples and blackberries from the garden Margaret and I made a nice crumble for lunch. Chagie came in the afternoon, very sympathetic. She's doing well at Bath HMV, and plans to buy a small car soon. After a tea, for which I had laid on some florentines, I drove her down to town to meet Clive and Youla.

In the car, I told Chagie of my dreams of loss, since they conveyed a cloaked reality. I wanted her to see beyond our cheerful façade to the cruel facts – and to know that I desired to communicate. Her silences are much like her mother's.

Today it rained and was cooler.

In the evening, Marcial Souto rang from the Argentine. I had to tell him of Margaret's illness. The poor sensitive man was struck dumb.

I can still touch her, kiss her, hold her slender hand, gaze into her eyes. But – it's our final summer together. I feel so bad, *devoured*. Is she – can she be as resigned as she makes out? I'm not resigned, merely torn apart.

Marcial asked me how old Margaret was. She is not given to repeating herself, but she said again today she had expected another twenty years of life.

Monday 25th August

She didn't sleep very well, in spite of sleeping pills and pain-killers. Bless her, she simply is not well, and maybe now will never feel any better. I couldn't drive her to Brighton, never mind France or Edinburgh, or the Ochils, not in her frail state.

I have to ring friends and tell them in a perfectly steady voice – Frank, Helge. But I don't wish to live without her. She is the better part of my life.

It rained all last night. Michael, of three doors away in Stoke Place, was in Wales. His house was broken into. The crooks levered open a front window. They did not steal much, leaving his three computers, for instance, so he declared himself only moderately pissed off. But the police called him back from Wales.

I was discussing the break-in with Hugh Ferris, who has bought the semi-detached house next door and is performing a remarkable DIY job on it, warning him to be sure and make his place secure against break-ins. An American neighbour, Kathy Garrard, in passing, said, 'In New York, they'd spray your walls with goddam paint . . .'

After a sleep, Moggins and I drove into town to drop notes in on Neil and Derek Johnson, our friendly accountant. Then I shopped in Budgen while M waited in the car. She is always

perfectly content there, resting, listening to the radio or one
of our Jug tapes. All the same, I worry that shopping takes so
long.

Jug music has formed a sort of leitmotif in our life
together. We were still unmarried when we drove off in a
Land-Rover for the Balkan country then called Jugoslavia.
There we toured for six months. Conditions were spartan,
which suited me, somewhat recalling my army days in India
and Burma. It was all new to well-brought-up Margaret
Manson, but she took to our nomadic life as to the manner
born.

Wherever we went we tried to listen to local music, or
buy records of it. Much of the beautiful folk music of
Jugoslavia carried Eastern echoes, from Turkey and the sorrows of the high Anatolian plain and beyond. When our
children came into the world, they would dance in our
living-room to the records we had collected.

There were modern popular tunes as well as folk.
Margaret had a liking for Predrag Gojkovic singing 'Kafu Mi
Draga Ispeci', which I suppose to mean 'Bring me some
coffee, darling'. The song has a slow dragging voluptuous-
ness. In camp sites and cafés we also heard a solemn deep
male voice singing a song we knew as 'Pod Moskovski
Večera'('Nights in Moscow'); rightly, Belgrade took Moscow
seriously. On our return to England, we found Kenny Ball
and his Jazzmen were playing a jollied-up version entitled
'Midnight in Moscow'. To hear it now is to recall our carefree roving days in a nation since vanished. It demolished
itself.

We felt safe there in the sixties, even when camping in wild places. In Tito's day, it was an orderly country. The Narodna Armie, the National Army, on the march permitted its soldiery to break ranks and pick wayside flowers. We laughed at that. Twenty years later, similar men were engaged in a genocidal war.

Looking back over our long years together, I see how Margaret and I forged our relationship in Jugland, depending greatly on each other, relishing our exile together.

Another upheaval in the family was the removal of Wendy and Mark from Victoria Road to rented accommodation in Bainton Road. Margaret and I were anxious about this move, considering Wendy's advanced state of pregnancy, but their plan was sound enough. It is so difficult to buy a house in North Oxford, particularly in a favoured school's catchment area, that you gain an advantage by having ready money; in that way, you are better equipped to compete for what comes on the market.

Clive and Youla were alone in Victoria Road, Wendy and Co. having driven up to Blakeney. We took them a cake, but they had already arranged a smart tea for us. We were glad to sit and talk to them. Although they flew from Athens to see how things were with us, we have seen all too little of them.

Moggins so sweet and precious today. A busy week ahead of us! New car, new shower, new house cleaners! She is preoccupied with sorting out various things, discarding some objects, trying to make future life tolerable for me. And hoping, of course, that our dear old kids will remember her.

As if they wouldn't . . .

Perhaps the unfortunate lady had in mind that alarming saying in Ecclesiastes: 'And some there be who have no memorial . . .' We all hope to achieve something, and Margaret achieved much. She need not have worried, if worry she did. She had never been the worrying kind.

Tuesday 26th August

Tim and Sarah turned up for lunch, loaded with goodies from Gluttons. M and I ate more than usual, to show willing. They were retrieving Sarah's car and returning the rented one, the Ka.

They were unable to stay long. Soon after they had gone, in rushed our new professional cleaning team. It was an alarming but comic performance as they whizzed round the house with their assortment of rags and polishes and liquids.

The older lady of the two sympathised with Margaret's illness. She is on the NHS and waiting to have a biopsy: 'The blood comes out of my poor old bottom.'

At least Margaret doesn't have to put up with that.

When they'd gone, the bell rang. There stood the pleasant-faced Kathy Garrard and her two children, paying a brief visit to see how Margaret was. The children were nice: bright, non-pushy and well behaved. I took them to play on one of the computers while Margaret and Kathy talked.

Jones arrived from the Antiques Centre and paid only £100 for one of our sofas, which he took away. By which time Moggins was fairly zonked, as she put it.

We received a touching e-mail from Lucia Elpi in Bologna

and a worrying letter from Petrushka, pregnant and suffering
from pre-eclampsia.

'Petrushka' was our pet name for our actress friend, Petronilla
Whitfield. It is strange how illness acts like a magnet for
news of other illnesses; or perhaps it was just that we had
entered the illness zone. Petrushka was pregnant with her
second child. She had had serious trouble with the first. If
you suffer from pre-eclampsia, your placenta is failing to
provide the infant with sufficient oxygen and food. She
found belatedly that this trait ran in her family.

Wednesday 27th August

*The pressure continues unabated, three or four people
or groups turning up each day. We must keep it quieter
next week. All very well intentioned and kind, though.*

*So poor B was up at 7.30 to open the door to Carters'
plumber Mike, who will replace the cramped old shower
next to our bedroom with a wider one with a fold-up
seat – excellent. But of course loads of banging and
crashing all day: Mike was finding it rather difficult to
do.*

*Then the new car was delivered! Such a delicious aqua
blue, so smooth inside and out!!*

*Sue Brack's gardener called round, a pleasant elderly
chap, very polite, who will try to fit us into his
schedule. Then B got worried about my breathlessness,
and called the doctor. Neil being away, Chris Kenyon
came up and B thought he was very good, as I have
found too.*

He listened to my lungs: apparently there's fluid there!
A dicky heart, crumbling liver and pancreas, and now
the lungs! Whatever next! So I add frusemide to my pills,
to make me pee the fluid away.

Later, Wm. Chislett brought Muriel [his mother]
round to visit; B had said only a quick half-hour, but
that was quite enough; my breathing troubled me;
neither of them said a word about being sorry to hear my
news.

Funny how people react, not knowing what to say or
do – flowers would have been acceptable (also from people
like Kay, I might have thought) . . . Anyway, it's difficult
for other people to take the news too. William at least
brought us a travel book on Spain, which I will enjoy.

So we took the new car into town to get my
prescription!! B drove very well, and we both greatly
enjoyed the outing!!

Total exhaustion later.

B made us another lovely supper, fish pie and orange
cheesecake; he's being brilliant at catering!

It was true I was getting the hang of shopping and of heating
pre-prepared food in the oven; but I wouldn't have put it
higher than that! Of course, there's the possibility that
Moggins put in these kind references to cheer me, knowing
I would come upon them when she was gone. We had a
habit of laying little snares of pleasure for each other.

The new Volvo was a wonderful gift; I took it to be M's
big, loving farewell present. An amiable man from
Motorworld delivered it, driving away in our old veteran.

Her breathlessness, to which she makes passing reference, was certainly a worry. Sitting in her customary spot on the sofa in the living-room, she could hardly speak without panting. Her Spanish fan remained ever at hand.

Among Margaret's callers were William Chislett and his mother. I had known William since he was a baby. They were very charming. William brought Margaret a friend's newly published book of travel. But neither mentioned Margaret's illness, which annoyed her. She complained about it when they had gone.

To be fair to Muriel Chislett, who is a good old friend of mine, she did exclaim, as I saw them to the gate and were out of earshot of Margaret, how terrible it all was, and how brave Margaret was being. Muriel belongs to a generation for whom the word 'cancer' was hardly to be spoken in decent company. Between us, Margaret and I made no bones about what ailed her. Nor did we seek to conceal it from others, or speak of it in hushed tones.

When I told someone what the matter was, they asked me, in tones of shock, 'Does Margaret know?'

Did she know?! Of course she bloody knew! But the question harked back to earlier times, when the nature of their disease was concealed from the dying patient. 'Oh, you'll be better soon, dear . . .' And so people faded out in a nest of lies. Such stratagems seem morally wrong now; but times change; and medicine improves, thank heavens.

Not that it has yet improved to the point where it could save Margaret's life. We have lived too soon.

These mornings, I had to get up early to let in Mike the plumber, a quiet, mild man. But I had developed a taste for early rising. That way, I earned myself a peaceful hour on the computer, revising the endless *Twinkling*, after taking Margaret her breakfast. No word came from my new publishers.

Margaret at this time held lengthy conversations on the phone with Wendy. They had long been allies. How considerate she was! Fearing that Wendy's energies were taxed, she conceived the idea of ordering our cleaners to clean Wendy's house as well, once a week, with us picking up the bill.

Friday 29th August
Another exhausting day! Yet it looked quiet according to the diary!

The plumber putting in our enlarged shower turned off & drained the boiler yesterday, and today could not get it going again. So we had to get Glowworm engineer to turn up – which he actually did within two hours!

Then B went off to Johnson's to get tiles and shower seat, and came back for a quick sandwich with me. I had meanwhile phoned a house clearance chappie to collect all the stuff we have been hoarding in the garage.

He finally turned up and wouldn't give us any money for any of it – the gent's wardrobe that had been in my bedroom at Gartmorn, and which recently, at Woodlands, Helen had painted and dragged in grey! The old desk dressing table that had been in the spare room downstairs which Grannie Manson used when staying with us, old bits of Wendy's, etc. etc.

He would take it all off our hands and mostly to the dump – so he said – if he could have our decent quality kitchen table (ex-Woodlands). In our present state, we were delighted to see everything go! Nothing like a good clear-out. So he stuffed most of it in his pick-up and took it away – hooray!

While B was bringing some Mars ice-creams back from Somerfield, the reflexology lady B had booked for me arrived, but I decided I wouldn't take her on at present because of all my medicaments, which are not yet doing their stuff. We asked if it was all right if B had the session instead. She agreed that I should not have it now, as the drugs might block 'the pathways', etc. etc.

At the same time, the new sofa arrived! It's some weeks after we paid for it, and B chased up the delivery most days! So two lads had to cart it into the sitting-room where B was being done, barefoot with his feet up!

Some lovely flowers arrived from Petrushka.

Surely we are nearly through all this madness – B is positively manic! We must slow down, or he will harm himself. He says he lost half a stone on hearing the bad news about me; I am now down to nearly 10 stone, from 11½.

Tomorrow Andy Durban comes to look at our finances, & B has a TV filming session in the evening, Clive & Youla stay overnight. Then the weekend is free!

I did try to keep the days free for us to live in peace, although that did not always work out. And Margaret enjoyed having a visitor in the afternoon. Someone with whom she could sit and talk cheerfully was good medicine for her.

The reflexology lady was a mixed success. I inherited her,

as Margaret explains. She was a laughing lady, well spoken, well informed. My feet were in her hands when in came two men bearing our delayed sofa. Delivered at last – paid for on 1st August.

My feet were extremely tender; paradoxically, dead yet hyper-sensitive. They needed treatment. When the lady dug her fingers into a particularly tender part, I yelped, where-upon she said in triumph, 'Ah, that's the hypothalamus!'

After a few visits with this treatment, I had to say, 'Look, lady, my hypothalamus is not troubling me. It's the feet that need solace.'

So she came no more. I rather missed her laughter.

We sat on the new sofa to eat our frugal supper, following a long phone call from a man on the *Financial Times*, who wanted to do a piece regarding Turkmenistan and my Makhtumkuli poems.

Another good e-mail from Dede. She knows what it's like.

Wendy phoned from the flat in Blakeney during the evening. She had taken Thomas to Thursford, to the jolly traction engine museum. Apparently there was a good man on the mighty wurlitzer.

Together with Mark, they had had coffee with Betty and Antony. Ant had followed them to the car and said something eccentric in Wendy's ear.

During this congested period, Clive and Youla had been stay-ing with Wendy and Mark. On Friday 29th August, they stayed with us overnight. Generally, when they were over from Athens, they were welcome here for as long as they liked; it was fun to have them. On this occasion, with Margaret's enfeebled and my overwrought state, it was not possible.

Clive was able to remain in England longer than intended because he was enjoying a sabbatical year from the British Council in Athens and they continued to stay at the Victoria Road house while Wendy was in Blakeney. I drove up in M's grand final gift to me and collected them.

I helped Clive and Youla concoct a large curry, of which Moggins managed to eat a good part of a plateful. Her digestive problems were slowly increasing. Nevertheless, my diary entry for that day reports that she seemed to be regaining some strength. She rose from bed a little earlier and retired a little later.

With every such hopeful sign, whatever my intellect told me, my emotions shouted, 'She's getting better! Hurray!'

Mike, Carters' plumber, finished his work after lunch. I gave him a bottle of wine by way of thanks. The new enlarged shower was a great improvement. The grouting would be dry enough for a quick inundation in the morning.

Punctilious Dr Kenyon phoned to see how Margaret was. A bouquet of flowers arrived from the publisher of her Boars Hill book. If only they would hasten and bring the book out . . .

Margaret was tired by sunset, and it was then – at nine in the evening – that Jane Rugoyska arrived with her camera crew for the shoot for Anglia TV. Why does one go through with these things? The knowledge that this was important to Jane helped considerably. I read my poem about insomnia to camera. I have every expectation that it will be cut. I introduced Clive to Jane.

She was keen to take night footage in the garden, away from Margaret's windows, and preferably with St Andrew's church tower visible in the background. Unfortunately, just as the crew were ready to go out, rain started coming down in sheets – in massive flock curtains, in fact.

Finally, a sodden little group bundled into their people-carrier at midnight, and drove damply away. Jane claimed they were going to film the dawn coming up.

What dawn, I wondered.

Next morning, the world was sodden.

Later it emerged that, as I had expected, my contribution was entirely cut from the programme. All the upheaval has been for nothing.

On that day, the last Saturday of the month, we drove to the nearby Potters in Larkins Lane. Jeremy lent Margaret a book entitled *Anatomy of an Illness*. She would not read it, saying it was intended for the healthy. She also refused to look at a posthumously published book of poems by a friend of ours, Jonathan Price's *Everything Must Go*. In this, she probably showed good sense. She had no need for anything to make her more miserable.

Jeremy was cheerful and feisty – a good encounter for Margaret. We stayed an hour, talking keenly. I felt compassion for Margaret Potter, knowing something of what she must be undergoing.

On Saturday we went round for a drink to the Potters:
Jeremy had bowel cancer diagnosed and was operated
on at the beginning of the year; it has now spread to his
liver. He seems so amazingly fit and cheerful, has no

pain, takes no pills, but says occasional things like 'I nearly thought I wouldn't be seeing September in.' Like me, he is finishing a book, and longing to see it through.

Margaret's book was a project on which she had been working for three years. It was nothing less than an historical anthology of life on Boars Hill. Margaret had long been expert in listening and recording conversations – sometimes long monologues – with inhabitants of that pleasant wooded area to the south of Oxford. These interviews were set in perspective by research she did in the county library and well illustrated by maps and photographs. Margaret continued to work on long after she became ill. She was fortunate to have devoted assistance from Patricia Simms, who finally saw into print the volume known as *A Boars Hill Anthology*.

Jeremy had no religious belief. He was a humanist. He laughed wryly about a vicar who talked to him regarding 'Death as a friend'. Death is the horrifying enemy of life for most people.

Sadly, this enemy came to Jeremy only two days after it had visited Margaret, a housebreaker and sneak-thief of people's happy lives . . .

I report that on the day we visited the Potters my darling patient enjoyed a visible improvement and an enhanced appetite. She breathed with less difficulty and gave every appearance of being happy.

Such respites were welcome, even when followed by a step down.

Allowed a little time to ourselves, we lay together on the new sofa, arms about each other. I gazed into her beautiful face, still unravaged. When she looked into my eyes, her irises were then deep blue. I read there such profound wordless love that for a moment I was entirely transported; a great charge of life ran through me. Despite all the misery since, that living moment remains when we looked on each other's souls. I think of it with pride. Tears spring to my eyes. I too become short of breath.

Oh yes, she loved me, loved me well. And she depended on me.

Perhaps one of the many trusting things her forceful gaze conveyed was this: You know I am entirely yours; now I will trust you to care for me until I become helpless and die.

Comfort Me, Sweetheart

'Oh, comfort me, sweetheart,
My years are behind me.
For I am now going
Where no man can find me.'

I gave my love a casket of silver
With its velvet lining showing.
'Place my heart in this, my darling,
Take it with you where you are going.'

Oh gone is my lover, whose arms once entwined me.
And darkness has fallen, as years fall behind me.

'Oh, the way's long and dreary
To go down the mountain.
There's no place to rest me,
No lodging or fountain.'

I gave my love a flask of chaste crystal
Like a pure snow cloud showing.
'Place my blood in this, my darling,
Take it with you where you are going.'

Oh gone is my lover, whose arms once entwined me.
And darkness has fallen, as years fall behind me.

'Oh, I fear for my journey
And the ills that now ail me,
With no one to ward off
The frosts that assail me.'

I gave my love the breath of my body
Like the warm south wind blowing.
'Wrap this round you, my darling,
To cloak you snugly where you are going.'

Oh gone is my lover, whose arms once entwined me,
Her light leads me onwards upon that same highway.
Alone I make my way
To meet her and greet her, my years all behind me.

[IV]

At the end of August, came a strange and unexpected occurrence. Margaret's and my lives had fallen into a routine, if a transitory one. She was, to a great extent, 'up and doing', as the saying goes, though more slow to rouse in the morning than had been the case with her usual spry self, who used to bring me tea. Now I rose first, came downstairs, switched on the radio, fed the cats, and took two mugs of tea back to the bedroom. Then I would shower, dress and come down to prepare Margaret's breakfast; at this time it consisted of a little cereal, or sometimes prunes, and a slice of Ryvita with honey.

On the Sunday morning of the last day of August, I omitted to switch on the radio. When I returned to the bedroom, Margaret was sitting up in bed. She had been listening to her bedside radio.

'Did you hear the news? Princess Di is dead!'

'What?'

It was hard to credit.

Diana and her lover, Dodi Fayed, had enjoyed a good free binge at the Ritz, after which their Mercedes crashed in the heart of Paris, supposedly trying to elude paparazzi on motorbikes. This beautiful, complex, in some ways mischievous, woman of thirty-six was unquestionably the most famous woman in the world. As the story unfolded throughout the day, it seemed that Britain and much of the rest of the world were in shock.

Hateful, brainless Death, killer of the young and beautiful, killer of beloved women!

We learned rapidly of the grief pouring out everywhere for the death of Princess Di. All this I read as mourning for my own beloved wife.

'No one can take her place,' people said.

Wendy and Mark arrived with Thomas during the evening. We had a pleasant time. I gave Thomas a box containing a hundred varied figures and animals. He played a game with Mark and me while Chris and Wendy talked.

'Now, Daddy and Grandpa, I don't want you to be scared, but here comes a yellow spaceman.'

We were terribly scared.

Monday, 1st September

Margaret and I, awake at 6.45, no longer wish each other 'Happy Month!' as invariably we had once done; we simply hoped we'd get by. I shuffle downstairs to get us some tea.

And meanwhile, a tsunami of raw emotion is washing over the country. Diana Princess of Wails has leaped from her smashed car straight into mythology, into sainthood.

The fact is, this self-styled 'ultimate rebel', as she flatteringly called herself, led an extremely privileged life, with frequent holidays abroad, massive shopping sprees and lackeys always at her command. No matter that she and Dodi had just had a good binge at the Paris Ritz (*buckshee*, presumably, since his pa owns the place), and she ('such a good mother . . .') hadn't seen her children for a month, so greatly was she enjoying this fling. No matter, she's now a saint, an angel.

Maybe she told their driver, mischievously, 'Let's give these bastards a run for their money!' – referring to the waiting paparazzi. They did not bother with seat belts, and off they went, aflame with love and wine.

In the apparently universal howl of mourning rising up, and the tonnage of flowers, there is something macabre, sexually greedy, vampiric. Everyone wants a share of the body.

Doesn't this display of grief demonstrate how sad are the lives of people in general, how lacking in love?

Clive and Youla came to see us in the afternoon, when Clive kindly volunteered to mow the lawn. Youla frisked about, making a game of it. We had tea together, and a cheerful chat. After which I drove them to Budgen – one of my new Meccas.

French police now report that Diana's driver was drunk 'three times over the limit'. I imagine they all were; but of that we are not told – it might induce a jarring note of realism into the orchestral broth of grief.

I fixed up an old TV set in the bedroom, so that Margaret could watch the news unfolding.

At this time she was still able to keep an intermittent record of events, although, as usual, saying little about herself.

Sunday 31st August

Wendy, Mark and Thomas turned up, fresh from Blakeney. Wendy looked really rested, just as well, as they are now into a heavy period when they have to move into rented accommodation in two weeks' time. Apart from all the work, I don't think Wendy is prepared for how much extra energy she will need for two kiddies, how very much

*Thomas will be upset at having a new 'intruder' into his
so-close relationship with Mummy. We volunteer to pay
for regular house-cleaning at least, so that the rented
house can be kept decent for them.*

Monday 1st September
   *I had an editorial meeting, with Trish, Wim
[Margaret's publisher] and son Daniel Meeuws, the latter
fresh back from four months in India and Ladakh, lucky
fellow. Wim is now primed to get going, everything to go to
the printer on 1st October, and with luck publication in
November! Great! We now have to insert the photos into
particular spots, which is a pleasant job I can do quickly.*
   *Also, Clive and Youla came round and cut the grass!
Good for Clive – it's ages since he did grass-cutting, and
he managed very well.*

Tuesday 2nd September
   *A nice quiet day. I sort out the filing on the floor and
hand it up to B, who learns to put it away in the right
spots, something he will have to now do with each letter
as he writes it – to save the horrid filing basket piling up!*

She makes no mention of Diana's death. Perhaps her per-
spectives were narrowing. Doubtless the word 'death' held
little personal attraction. Yet we were fairly buoyant at this
time, this tiny period of time: not yet out on the ultimate
peninsula. She was still coolly continuing to edit her book,
placing the illustrations where she wanted them.
   I note on the first of the month:

Moggins still pants alarmingly, but seems better in some other ways. She was cheerful when hosting an editorial meeting on the Boars Hill book here, with Wim Meeuws and Trish. I stayed out of the way, apart from getting them coffee. (Water for Moggins; she sips her Volvic all the while.)

This evening, she enjoyed the supper I prepared, courtesy of Sainsbury's, chicken and ham pie with savoy cabbage and new potatoes, followed by blackberry and apple pie with *crème fraîche*.

And she was still occupied with putting her affairs in order. She was methodical; her disposition never changed. The 2nd of September was beautiful, crisp and fresh. The heatwave had died, the flies had quit the kitchen, the bouquets were piling up outside Kensington Palace.

I got the washing out early on the line – something that still has novelty value. Margaret remained in bed a while, turning out letters, cards, memorials of her yesterdays – her pleasant and placid yesterdays, so different from mine. Her old Covent Garden programmes, many of them signed by the celebrated singers of the time, are spared from the general destruction. She does it all so cheerfully, like a young girl preparing for a party. I sit on the bed, admiring her. Oh, her delicate wrist movements, her quick glances, the pleasure of her presence . . .

I can't bear to see how well and carefree we were, just a few weeks ago.

The same melancholy thought occurred to Margaret, who was in reflective mood on her computer at this time.

Friday 5th September

About a month since we learned the news. We do not speak of the future, about how things might deteriorate, about what B will do afterwards, etc. We concentrate on my day-by-day health, today rather better I believe, on a double dose of fluid-removing pills, frusemide, to take away excess fluid in the lungs.

Less panting and sweating.

Some days better than others: yesterday afternoon poor B was totally exhausted, having accompanied me into Phillips auctioneers to have jewellery, Alma-Tadema and carriage clock valued and put in for sale. The day before he had wretched trouble with the car with a flat battery, but survived it calmly and without swearing: not so yesterday. Poor chap, this does take its toll on him. Today he woke at seven and brightly went down to make us tea. It should have been me looking after him in the normal course of events.

Friends being so kind and sweet. A lovely letter from David Wingrove today [*David is the writer friend who collaborated with me on* Trillion Year Spree].

During this period – which I would not call taxing, so much as full of ominous change, although emotionally taxing, of course – we had no additional help, apart from the fortnightly incursions of the cleaners.

We seemed to manage all right as long as we remained at home and were not too besieged by visitors.

Certainly the visit to the auctioneers was a strain. I have a mistrust of auctioneers, estate agents and funeral directors;

one is always at their mercy, and a butt of their secret scorn. My description of the auction rooms is less generous than Margaret's.

Afternoon: following a sleep, off to Phillips auctioneers, their seedy labyrinthine premises, with M's crown jewels and my old suspect Alma-Tadema. Might as well flog it. It looks pretentious in Hambleden; it was fine in Woodlands and better still in Heath House, where its grand gilt frame echoed the Corinthian pillars of the porch. We had to kick about in the corridor; found a chair for Moggins, who could not stand for long. No arrangements. Over an humiliating hour there in the stuffy place. Chaps practising contempt. Then buzzing round town, traffic, red lights. Bought a wedding anniversary card for Wendy and Mark, and a book, Damasio's *Descarte's Error*. M patient as usual. Got home, both thoroughly fatigued.

By then, almost time to start worrying about supper. M helped.

But we were slipping, slipping, into another phase.

I begin to realise how helpless she is. She begins brightly, but it takes her an hour to wash and dress. The new shower is useless for her. She has become so delicate that the sprinkling water hurts her flesh.

Coming downstairs, she sits and pants, resting on several steps, laughing it off if I come to help.

The doctors are away somewhere. O God, what can we do?

Lunch, then she sleeps on the sofa. We like the sofa, stylish but comfortable, and have ordered another, identical but with different covering. Hope it comes soon.

Then she's better. She sits sweetly, looks lively, but makes no move to get up, smiles, and laughs prettily when receiving visitors.

Nice visitors. Today, Edith and David Holt. David is recovering well from his heart attack. They are so amiable. I serve tea.

Postcard today from Roger and Vanessa in Copenhagen. M and I recognise the kind of pretty corner depicted, and regret we'll never visit that pleasant city again.

Too hectic a day to describe. Too many phone calls. Too much. I'm weary. Some Metaxa and a look at the news on the box.

I grieve because I can spend so little of her alert time with her. At night my nervous system demands a period in solitude, no phones, no tasks. When I do go upstairs, she is almost always asleep. I look at her and think . . . It can't be said what I think.

In the outer world, thousands, millions are making a show of grief for Princess Di. It's macabre.

They don't weep for my Moggins, who has always worked so hard. Di's stints of doing good were interspersed with the normal occupations of the rich and privileged: frequent trips abroad, massive shopping sprees, banquets, abounding holidays, the best of everything.

It might have been at this time, when the weather was less burdensome, that Margaret experienced a slight remission. Perhaps at this stage she still hoped to live until Tim's wedding in May. Perhaps she still hoped to wander again in the

Ochils. And perhaps I still believed, despite everything, that she was going to recover – to shrug it off, and laugh and say 'Let's go to France to celebrate!' in the manner of her old carefree days.

I am out of touch with my own feelings, and mystified by Margaret's cheerfulness. It makes me feel at times I really do not know her. I know I contain anger. She must surely be angry too, at this monstrous cheat, in some level of her being. We play out our choked lives against a week when Britain seems to have gone mad with grief for the death of Princess Di.

People stand for hours, toting flowers, weeping, signing endless volumes of remembrance. For someone they never knew. 'All for nothing! For Hecuba! What's he to Hecuba, or Hecuba to him, that he should weep for her?'

Here, it's different. These strange crowds, not just here but in foreign towns, for all I know in the Upper Nile, in Luxor as in London, stand and drip woe, and encroach on our right to grieve in private.

Friday 5th September

How long we still have together I cannot make out. No one will or can say. Neil came this afternoon. He didn't say.

He examined Margaret quite thoroughly. She does seem better than she was – and says so. She put on the oven to heat today, and dried dishes (sitting down) while I washed up our supper dishes. These simple companionable things . . .

Neil juggled her pills. I drove to collect her prescribed phamaceuticals from Hornby's, and also copped a £20 parking

ticket for parking for five minutes on a double yellow line in
Old High Street.

We're much together. I make her bed, she makes her phone
calls.

Clive's in London. I hope to see him tomorrow.

This week, with its brief broken days, has been played out
against the strange phenomenon of rabid mourning for
Diana's death – about which questions remain to be answered.

At least we are not alone in our revulsion against the
lachrymose fit by all and sundry. A reader in the *Independent*
writes, 'I cannot believe the mass hysteria sweeping the nation.
Every radio station, newspaper and television station is
torturing us with their exaggerated sorrow. There must be
some other news worth reporting.'

Quite right, sir! There's a lady dying over here, sir!

My cousin John Wilson rang to say that Stella, his wife,
has had a mild stroke. We sent her flowers. Poor Stella has
endured much suffering recently.

Saturday 6th September

A beautiful cool sunny day. Blue skies over London.
Hundreds of thousands of people line the route taken by
Diana's funeral cortège. Perhaps they mourn for Diana,
perhaps for themselves, that their life is not what they would
wish, that they, like her, suffer from low self-esteem.

Elton John was allowed to sing a very tacky song, a retread
of an earlier one, in Westminster Abbey. Diana must have been,
in the words of a Red Cross worker, 'a very special person'.
Closer to home is another very special person, still in bed.

Moggins is okay this morning. When I went up last night, she was breathing heavily and noisily, rather in bursts. She had taken sleeping pills, so I did not like to wake her, although I was alarmed. Neil had prescribed a different sleeping pill. I could not sleep, and my right leg bothered me. Later in the night, she became quiet, as if exhausted.

We enjoyed a peaceful day, with Moggins feeling quite a lot better. I did not have to shop – and in any case the shops were closed for the funeral. We watched a lot of the ceremony on TV, weeping once or twice.

Margaret talked about walking in her garden again – a hopeful sign. I wondered if we could fly to the lovely little Hotel du Port on the southern shores of Lake Geneva. We have been so happy there in the past. Maybe in two weeks?

Clive and Youla sailed in cheerfully for tea, bringing with them a tasty strawberry tart. Clive showed us photos of Amorgos, which they had recently visited. How tranquil the island looked, how inviting the sea! It's unlikely we shall reach the Aegean again.

We ate well and were as happy as could be.

Quiet day for us, historic for England.

So many sad people in the world.

My judgement was at fault. She said she felt better; but that was not the case.

Sunday 7th September

Over the weekend I was not so good, Neil changed the pills a bit, and it made me much more feeble. Talked to him on the phone on Monday and we went back to the previous dose. He is obviously as puzzled by the heart-rate and panting as B and I are.

If I could shake that off I should be fine; in good spirits and longing to walk round the garden. He's going to call again on Thursday.

Jill Stallworthy came round yesterday, B will be having lunch with Jon at Green College – the first time he will use his Common Room membership! Jill is sweet, easy to chat to, quite unmade-up and no sort of hair-do. Informal, sympathetic and nice. Now we await the two-night visit of Bet & Ant, staying at a guest house up the road. Great effort on their part to come down; especially as Ant is in a non-eating phase again. Quite ghastly, especially for Betty.

I chase up Wim and Daniel Meeuws, who do not seem to read their e-mails; we need action now on which photos to put in the Boars Hill Book, and it must go to the printer on 1st October – must must must!

Stilted letter from Sammy Lundwall, addressed only to B. It's the 'does he take sugar' syndrome. But I e-mailed them and both he and Ingrid wrote lovely separate letters!

Now her entries were growing shorter and came at longer intervals. There was nothing but sorrow to relate.

Sunday 7th September

The sun umbrella is put away, the sun chairs from the helix are locked away in the summerhouse. I cannot check my tears: the last summer she and I will ever share has faded and gone.

I weed the paths and give them a good brush.

Although Margaret was less energetic, we had a pleasant
day. I shopped in the morning, feeling strange that it no
longer seemed wrong to be shopping on a Sunday.

Charlotte came in the afternoon. She was rather
overwhelmed by her mother showing her jewellery she will
inherit, together with the documents in which M has
methodically recorded all our financial arrangements.

M is much occupied in preparing and making
straightforward everything for her absence; how typical of her
to care for us all.

I feel so sorry for our dear Chagie, in losing her mother; she
was so sad and serious as I drove her into town. Our sweet
youngest offspring; her feelings are so tender. She wishes, and
we wish, that she was still working in Oxford. Not that Bath is
exactly at the ends of the Earth.

If we mourned quietly in our house in Old Headington,
beyond our walls a great hullabaloo of grief still continued for
Princess Diana.

Although the ceremonies at Westminster Abbey were
touching, the adulation heaped on the poor woman was
alarming. Diana loved the miserable, the unfortunate, yet
was a greedy person. I cut out an extract from an article by
Aminatta Forra in the day's *Independent*. According to Forra,
Diana had asked too much, as well as wanting contradictory
things. She wanted, for instance, to be a traditional mother to
her sons, and an independent woman. After transforming
herself into an alluring beauty, she demanded to be left alone.
She disliked the Press, yet flirted with it.

Diana suffered from an ailment peculiar to the modern

Western world, where a new generation regard the pursuit of personal happiness as a birthright, and are unprepared for the consequences of devoting oneself to the pleasure principle.

Although this is a generalisation, it has general application. I could but contrast it with Margaret, who found happiness in her own modest sphere, who was not self-seeking, and whose success within her own defined orbit had granted her a lucidity, an equanimity, that was to survive until she died.

Monday 8th September

Moggins felt very unwell today. Extremely disappointing. The balance of steroids is not right. She experienced great difficulty showering, dressing and simply getting downstairs. She panted heavily. I helped her into the living-room, where she lay on the sofa gasping.

Agony for her. And for me, the bystander.

Looking back in these notebooks, I was forced to realise she has been unwell for several months. If only we had twigged sooner! But little good that would have done; pancreatic cancer is almost always inoperable. Any weakness she suffered was ascribed to her heart condition, which had become almost a routine matter. How long do these things take?

I found myself very tense, with a rapid irregular heartbeat. Unfortunately, I had asked Jon Stallworthy to lunch with me in Green College; but it was an enjoyable occasion in the event, and Jon was his usual pleasant self.

After a post-prandial sleep, Margaret was a little better. We hung about. I stuffed some washing into the washing machine.

Weatherwise, it was a beautiful day, calm and sunny. So I

helped brave Moggins into the new car and we went shopping.
We called in on Wendy, Mark and Thomas in Victoria Road; it
was their thirteenth wedding anniversary. They were super as
usual. They had all been to inspect the house they will rent in
Bainton Road. Clive seemed pleased with it.

But Margaret did not feel strong enough to leave her seat
in the car.

And that was the sort of routine into which our life then fell,
if only for a brief period. Margaret slowly grew weaker; but
there were days when she felt a little better, and then we
hoped again: or, to be more accurate, I could not help hoping
again. What Margaret inwardly believed I did not know.
Although we communicated constantly by speech, touch,
looks of love, we dared not venture over that dark threshold
of the future. She set an embargo on it, perhaps in order to
maintain her equilibrium. Still she did what she could, and
planned for her anxious family.

In one of my fits of needing reassurance, I tried to ring a
Macmillan nurse, without letting Margaret know I was doing
so, thinking it would only indicate how worried I was. The
nurse rang back. Unfortunately, I was then up in the bedroom with Margaret. She answered the call on her cordless
phone.

'It's my call!' I kept telling her. She did not pass the phone
over. The nurse told her she would come on the following
day.

I was annoyed. 'I did keep telling you it was my call.'

'I thought you were saying "Michael".'

'Why would I be saying that?'

'I couldn't understand what you were going on about when the nurse was speaking in my ear.'

The time was coming when Clive and Youla would have to return to Athens. Clive's belongings were distributed in various stores, and in his sister's house. I helped them move his valuables, and took over several boxes of things to store here in our spare room – Charlotte's room, which has become a glorified box-room. Clive was, as ever, equable and pleasant.

When I returned home, there was my darling girl, sitting at her computer, smiling, giving me a wave of greeting, as she had always done. Seeing her there – although it might be growing late – how could I believe she, *she* of all people, would soon die? And what illusion was she under at that moment.

It was a fine day, with bright sun and no breeze. Margaret wore one of her pretty summer dresses. I went in and kissed her. If only such moments might remain, embalmed in time . . .

That day, Betty and her husband Antony arrived from Norfolk. It was quite brave of them to come, since Antony is no fan of long drives. I worried about what my sister might think, and if she would be upset. She remarked later that Margaret's face was thinner; seeing that dear face every day, I had not noticed.

No sooner had they arrived, than Roger Carter came – to be followed by young Meeuws, Margaret's publisher's son. Betty calmly got us some tea, while I dealt with Roger and Margaret tackled Junior.

My scheme, such as it was, was always to think of some small thing that would draw Margaret's thoughts ahead to practical matters.

We had inherited two horrible wooden doors in the kitchen. In their time, they had served as rafts for the *Medusa*. They had iron latches, and were an inheritance from the days when the house had been a Victorian cottage. One stood between the kitchen and dining-room. Moreover, the other one, between the kitchen and the hall passage, would not shut properly; it did not fit. And no one had cared for a hundred years . . .

I wanted these two doors replaced by good doors with frosted glass panels, leaded to match the external windows – two doors that would open and close in the customary manner of doors. So Roger measured up and made sensible suggestions regarding style.

It would please Margaret.

In the event, the doors were hung only the day before Margaret went into Sobell House. Clinging to my arm, she was able to inspect and admire them . . . But really they were too late.

It was extremely agreeable to have Bet and Ant with us. They were amusing as usual, and Margaret enjoyed their company. I made them a good supper; even Antony, always in trouble with food, ate some of the fish pie. Later on, when Margaret went slowly up to bed at 8.30, I drove them to their bed and breakfast hotel, The Dial House, on the London Road. We did not lend them our guest room; I was unable to face having other people, even close relations, in the house.

Returning here, I slumped in front of the television to watch the movie of Robert Harris's alternative world novel, *Fatherland*.

At this time, Abigail Hatherley, the daughter of my old friend Frank Hatherley, was setting to music a poem I had written, 'When You are Gone'. This was a secret to surprise Margaret. When the CDs arrived, I found what a beautiful song Abigail had made of it, but did not dare give it to Moggins, since it would only have made her miserable. Besides, she knew very well that I would be utterly desolate when she was no longer here.

When You Are Gone

When you are gone –
Everything unnatural will strike the Earth.
    Orifices will be clogged,
The skies will never clear.
One-year-olds will give violent birth.
Forests will burn and deserts be waterlogged.

When you are gone –
Cars will no longer steer
Their course along motorways:
They'll park among the Himalayas.
Sweaty men in dark suits
Will never drink down pints of beer,
The Pope will fart during prayers.
O Love, all music will disappear,
So for ever the noise of Bach
Will rest among the forbidden fruits,
Along with kisses, picnics, and such pursuits.

Monstrosities will be born.
There'll be no sons or daughters.
Those who walk the streets will neither see nor hear,
Bailiffs will confiscate their sexual quarters.
Tinnitus will afflict the ears of corn.
Earth will lose its atmosphere.

When most hated is what was most dear –
When you're gone – there'll be no cakes
Or ale, or things the baker bakes.
Lovers will no longer cling
Or laugh at their secret jokes
As we have done. Those small birds overhead
Will drop dead in flight. By night
The cockroach will sing,
'Pity, pity, pity . . .'

Things will go from bad to worse.
When the Moon falls from the sky
Crushing some god-forsaken city,
Then I'll know you've gone,
Pulling the plug on the universe.
I'll remain to wonder why –
Scarcely a man, a troll, a Caliban.

[V]

This is a sad enough tale of decline; yet I was, in a way my wife could not know, sustained by the drama of it. My adrenalin count was high. Only when the coffin was lowered into the ground and the mourners had departed, and no guests called at the house, and the flowers wilted in their vases did that sustaining power ebb. Then the real emptiness entered.

Yet there are many men who would envy my condition, who never knew such a sweet-natured lady. And even for those without the consolation of religion, there must come a sense that our time is eternal, that a part of our life lives in another dimension, and that beyond the confines of our mortal lives somewhere a trace of our spiritual journey remains, as lovers' initials carved on a living tree remain after they are dead. Life, like light, travels fast. Light, except in local planetary conditions, is hard to extinguish. To express this intuition of continuity, we have to turn to unscientific and holy persons, such as the anchoress Julian of Norwich, who claimed 'All shall be well and all shall be well and all manner of thing shall be well . . .' Positive, if a bit vague.

But perhaps nearer to my meaning is a thought expressed in the *Bhagavad Gita*: 'We all have been for all time; I, and thou, and those kings of men. And we all shall be for all time, we all for ever and ever.' Or perhaps it is that love seems to transcend the limits of our brief mortal lives, and is carved into the living trees of other people.

The day before Clive and Youla flew back to Athens, most

of the family gathered here in Hambleden. Much happiness in consequence. It had not been easy for Clive, although we had seen something of each other. I was much comforted by their kindness.

As they left, they had been very clever and secretly left Chris and me big surprises; these we found when I took her tea up to bed. Her surprise was a wooden tray with legs, ideal for meals in bed – the more generous since they had already bought her a woollen bed jacket. My surprise was an elaborate Cassio watch. My old digital, worn for at least twenty years, was on its last legs. Why, it would no longer even play 'The Yaller Rose of Texas'. The Cassio, also a preferred digital, has many additional features; it can, for instance, list fifty telephone numbers, although I have not yet had the courage to try out this facility. I was thrilled – not least by their thoughtfulness.

During that evening, Neil called. Margaret had seemed stronger, and was in good fettle, but complained to the doctor about her bad heart flutter. Neil said he would book another appointment with Dr Hart.

When that appointment came, I drove her to the hospital's cardiology department. There, five terminals were taped to her breasts. She had to wear the machine for twenty-four hours, during which time it would record her heart patterns. We hoped some good would come of it.

As I pushed her round the floors of the John Radcliffe, I said to her, 'At least you have a loving spouse to care for you.'

She replied that she had always expected to look after me in my old age.

'But the family will look after you, darling,' she added.

I hoped I would never become a burden to them. I had not thought that far ahead. I was still fairly sprightly, but when I became incapacitated – well, it was a gloomy prospect if you stopped to think about it, and thinking was not going to help greatly.

The potassium pills were not having their expected beneficial effect. Margaret grew weaker. Oh, what misery, what happiness, was that time!

I wished into my diary that if only we could live for ever just as we were then, with my darling frail but content, and I making the meals and doing the work, then it would be perfect happiness. She sits quietly, stroking her favourite Sotkin or reading one of many magazines I bring her, which seem to hold her interest, *Country Living, Homes and Gardens, Country Life* and the like.

She had always enjoyed *Country Life*. She was fascinated by the range and diversity of houses on offer for sale, a wide selection of the British inheritance of love of home on small or grand scale.

In our early married life, we had frequently moved. As a writer, I was not tied to one place. And Margaret loved planning colour schemes, making curtains, transforming gardens. Just when we were settled comfortably somewhere, Margaret would start buying *Country Life* once more. Her migratory instincts were rousing again . . .

Margaret's diet steadily declined. The prunes-at-breakfast phase came and went. Then it was bananas, then none. No toast. Tea had disappeared from the menu. Her breakfast became for a while cereal and a glass of milk. Sometimes, she pushed it away, unable to eat. She took a pain-killer instead.

Oh, how she looked at me this morning! What did that dear long look say? 'I know I'm dying and I'm sorry for your sake?' My sweetest girlie, if only it was I making my last bow and *you* were well and free to go blithely about the world as once you did!

Other minor matters plagued me. I attempted to print out *Twinkling*. I was sick of the book, with which I had already been dealing for three years, and was aware I had not cut or altered enough. A short way through the print-out, the toner dried up. I had to visit Absolute Computers and buy another cartridge.

The bloody manuscript takes up 650 double-spaced pages. That's a quarter of a million words long.

On that day in the middle of September, Patti Pugh the Macmillan nurse arrived. I had phoned for her in desperation. She was the nurse we had met on our visit to Sobell House, a stout trooper – and a compassionate one. She stayed with us for almost an hour. We were able to talk frankly about the cancer, which afforded us some consolation.

At one point she asked Margaret, 'Are you afraid?'

Margaret thought a little and then said firmly, 'No.' I was very proud of her. I was the one who got the whim-whams.

Patti was so capable that we were encouraged.

But I was haunted by the fear that the cancer might be far advanced. We did not know how much longer she could continue, happy but badly handicapped. She had never at this point managed to walk as far as our new flowerbed, which we had planned together, and in which dahlias now bloomed, the deep red Bishops of Llandaff.

We returned to the cardiology department in the JR. Getting there was a performance, procuring one of the hospital's clumsy wheelchairs, manoeuvring it along corridors, etc. But eventually Margaret had a heart-to-Hart talk with the pleasant doctor.

Her heart had hypertrophied under high blood pressure. An exact understanding of how these tribulations came about escaped us. During such interviews, one is naturally anxious, which is not conducive to taking in a string of technical details.

Dr Hart was encouraging, but the news was poor. He prescribed flecainide, which we went down and bought immediately at the JR pharmacy. It was a hot day. Margaret suffered from a long wait at the counter. We could only hope that the new drug would have a beneficial effect.

This was all so awful for Margaret. Good news was never going to reach her ears again.

The fine weather continued. At a time of crisis, fine weather – sun, stillness – assumes a waiting quality, making the time more hard to bear. Since it seemed we had no future, we talked together about our past. As friends came and went, leaving behind them trails of good wishes, wine, cakes, flowers, chicken pies and books, Margaret greeted them all warmly. She talked to them, I thought, with gracious command, fluently and easily, and without self-consciousness.

And that made me happy, for I had known her when it was not so. We spoke about those times. Margaret herself recalled the shy and silent little thing she once was, inept at personal relationships because of a reserve she could not break through. When we knew each other in our early days, a teasing friend had called me a Svengali. But no, I loved her from the start, and so I had listened to her, and cared; it was I who had taught her to talk and be confident.

In return, she had taught me much, and made me a better person. We were immeasurably indebted to each other.

This is what it means to say I loved her from the start. I was in the old offices of the *Oxford Mail* in New Inn Hall Street, when the paper was a broadsheet. On the day Margaret arrived to act as secretary to the editor, I happened to see her coming along the corridor. She was wearing a light tweed coat, unbuttoned. She held herself beautifully, walking smartly, looking neither grim nor exuberant: a slender lady with her head held slightly to one side.

She gave the impression of a modest person, slightly and becomingly shy, but determined. That first impression remained with me, truthful and clear. It sustained me, even when we had our severe falling out in the late seventies. I liked what I saw then; it might be claimed that I knew instinctively that this was the girl for me.

The friend of ours, Petronilla, with whom I had been acting in *SF Blues*, was delivered, by emergency Caesarean of a small boy. He weighed only just over 3lbs, and was in intensive care. We sent flowers. There were only weeks to go before Wendy's son was born. She and Mark and Thomas began to move into the Bainton Road house. And Wendy was still working . . . We agonised about that.

When she could, Margaret still spent the odd hour in the study. It was not only her sweet, calm presence that would be missed, but her efficiency and business acumen. She had been shrewd, for many years keeping neat accounts of cash flow; she managed our investments well, in conjunction with Andy Durban and our accountant Derek Johnson. It was thanks to her that we were not too hard up, despite the marked diminution of literary income at that time.

As to that diminution, I had some books in the pipeline. Like Mr Micawber, I hoped that something would turn up.

Neil visited Margaret. He often came fairly late in the evening, making light of the hour by saying he was on call anyway. He announced that there was no longer fluid in her lung; the diuretics had cleared it. We were thankful for small mercies.

Neil also prescribed quinine pills for my legs. They worked for a while.

> I woke feeling refreshed and pretty cheerful. 'Well, things are not too bad . . . I can hang on here for a bit', etc . . . Everything passes through the mind.

Margaret's mood never seemed to change, although she varied between being alive and being half-dead. Whereas I went from blackest mood to wild fits of elation. However, since I concealed my mood swings from her as much as possible, we must suppose she concealed hers from me.

When I was most hard-pressed and would have to go and shop at a supermarket, which was still something of an ordeal, I would get into the car and insert a CD of Gregorian chanting; immediately a mood of sensuous calm would descend on me. A strange thing when one was roasting in hell!

On one of her better days – oh, there were worse to

come, but in September there were still good times – I drove her to see Wendy and Mark's new home. It was a pleasant house, with views across the St John's playing fields. Wendy was cheerful as ever and Thomas not too boisterous. In fact, he showed me round the house, explaining everything. Later I read to him from Henri Troyat's *Life of Pushkin*.

Margaret seemed well enough to be escorted to the Phoenix Cinema to see *Mrs Brown*, with Judi Dench playing Queen Victoria and Billy Connolly – an old favourite of ours, whom we had met – playing her Highland servant John Brown. The photography in itself was a pleasure. Margaret was comfortable throughout and enjoyed the film: fortunately, since this was to be her last visit to the cinema.

After the film, we bought a takeaway curry at the new Bagischa restaurant in North Parade. Margaret could eat little of it.

On the following day, she seemed rather worse and was dull. The flecainide was not having the desired effect. She gasped when she talked. We had a quiet day.

And the day after that. Worse again. The gardener came: £25. The cleaners came: £44. I shopped at Sainsbury's and ran up a big bill. It worried me that I always bought too much and always had to throw food away. Margaret ate less and less. And drank more and more of the little bottles of mineral water.

She remained feeble and sleepy all that day. When going up to bed early, she took sixteen small paces from the sofa in the living-room and collapsed on the chest in the hall.

'Oh God!' she exclaimed in misery. I helped her up the stairs. One step. Then another. Then one more. The wretchedness, the helplessness . . .

Alone downstairs – but I was not alone because she was alive upstairs; later, I would more fully understand what *alone* meant – I switched on the news. It showed shots of Kuching, that pretty and pleasant capital city of Sarawak, where I had been. Not so pretty now, being smothered in smoke. It seemed as if Sumatra and half of South-East Asia was on fire.

Friday 26th September

She was a little better, but still decidedly more feeble than last week. Why can't I face it, my dear lady love is *just bloody ill* . . . In the afternoon, I managed to coax her out of the living-room door a few steps on to a cushioned bench in the helix. There we sat together for five minutes, mute, in the thin sunshine . . .

She also sat in the kitchen with me and gave me advice on cooking little lamb chops for supper. And she taught me to make a white sauce to serve over the cauliflower. We had to laugh at my ineptitude. When the meal was served she could eat little enough of it.

Neil arrived after I had cleared away. Seeing how she was, he prescribed a double dose of this lousy flecainide. I'll get the stuff from Hornby's in the morning.

Neil had a glass of wine with me. When I escorted him to the side gate, I asked how long he thought Margaret had had the cancer. He replied, 'Quite a while, maybe a year.'

As I feared. A year ago in Cascais: she already had it then, I'm sure. She was ill then, but we didn't know how ill.

What did I say to Neil?

But he said, 'She'll not be better. But she could last out till Christmas . . .'

Christmas! Oh no. That's only three months away . . .

I had to recover myself before I went back to her.

How am I going to break this to the rest of the family, to prepare them?

They have their own lives to be lived. Best to keep this ghastly snatch of information to myself. *Christmas* . . .

She did so long to see Tim married in May. *May!* You might as well say 'married on Jupiter', it's so distant.

'If you want to love, you have to accept the pain' – my old friend C.S. Lewis.

[VI]

All of South-East Asia was going up in smoke. It seemed more fitting than the gnashing of teeth for Princess Diana's death. From Sumatra to the Philippines, and as far north as Kuala Lumpur, the smoke pall extended. It must have seemed, in those parts, that the whole world was on fire. As Shakespeare says in *Julius Ceaser*,

When beggars die, there are no comets seen;
The heavens themselves blaze forth the death of princes.

Saturday, 27th September

Margaret's pulse rate was 100 – far too fast.

So today the diuretic is off; it clashes with the flecainide acetate. I was up at Hornby's by 9.15 and Moggins was swallowing the first pill by 9.35. These are 100-gram pills, twice the dose of the first lot we bought in the JR. How may pills has she now let rattle down her long-suffering throat? To what effect?

Well, let's hope these will do some good.

In truth, she was better by a degree over yesterday. The weather was fine, we drove out to Millett's Farm, to buy and eat a picnic lunch there. It's now settled I drive the 850; Margaret has not been at the wheel. We remained in the car in the sun. She ate a yoghurt.

I wheeled her round the garden centre to buy some spring bulbs. Spring, ha! How typical of her brave spirit to think that far ahead, or to think that I, seeing those tender plants in flower, might dwell on her memory and recall her face and touch when she was alive. And her tender care of me, for so many vanished years.

We were out for some time, buying Mark some Austin Reed tokens for his birthday, some Nurishment from Budgen, and typing paper from Office World. Now that *Twinkling* is off my hands, I'm having to press on with *White Mars* as best I can.

For supper I cooked a fisherman's pie, with savoy cabbage and potato. Margaret ate quite well by her standards. She looked livelier and seemed happier. You get used to anything. We have almost changed roles! But sometimes there's a dimness in the gaze of her eyes . . .

Sunday 28th September

4 a.m. Sometimes when I go up to bed, she is breathing with such labour, her mouth open, making a sad noise. But just now I was woken by her silence. Her breathing is barely discernible; nor did she rouse or stir as I moved about. Fear seized me that her gallant heart had failed and she had died in her sleep, without a farewell.

In the morning, I must write to Tim and warn him how short the time may be in which we can enjoy her living presence amongst us. I much doubt that she can survive to be at his wedding in May.

Perhaps Tim can warn Chagie. She might take it better from her brother than from me.

How little, how very little, Moggins deserves this suffering.

She is still reading Lisa St Aubin, etc. I found her two of her novels, one of which she finished this morning. I cooked a chicken! Fortunately, hens come with instructions on their bottoms nowadays; any number can play. I served it with sausages and bread sauce. Moggins pleased by the effort but could eat little. Her throat is so dry, despite all the water she has to drink. She has ceased to take the diuretics. She did eat a little lemon meringue pie.

Chagie arrived in time to help me wash up. The day was so nice; we drove over to see Wendy and Mark in their new house. They seemed fairly calm, despite Thomas making a terrible row, rushing about clashing coconut shells. A bit much for Margaret to take.

We had tea and tried to talk.

Chagie came back here with us. She spoke with her dear mama. I was touched to see how lingeringly they embraced when saying farewell. Walking my poor daughter to the gate, I cuddled her while she cried a little on my shoulder. I had to say to her that she should not be misled by her mother's brightness in the brief times they were together: life for the dear lady was increasingly a struggle. I softened it by not mentioning the Christmas aspect.

Poor sweet Chagie! She says she thinks about it all the time.

Naturally enough, children see their mothers from a perspective very different from their father's point of view. A lover's experience differs markedly from a child's. Perhaps they tend to think of Margaret as rather saintly. Certainly she was the best of mothers to them, always patient and considerate to all four. But I would do her an injustice if I did not mention her passionate nature, which perhaps became less evident in our later years.

In the early stages of a marriage, some settling in has to be done. This took the form in our case of occasional plates and saucers being hurled at me and cups of coffee thrown over me. What I had done on such occasions escapes me, but not the glorious vitality with which they were flung. It was a novelty; not enjoyable exactly, but more bracing than having one's partner going off into sulks for a day or two. And the plate act was counterbalanced by the alacrity with which, at the touch of a caressing hand in the right place, she would rush upstairs to the bed with me.

One of her characteristics was to be open emotionally and yet to be private about herself and her past history. My anecdotes, humorous or grim, about my past found no counterpart in her. She needed a certain distance of her own, her 'own space', as people say nowadays.

It was important not to question her, not to question each other. It followed that she was no gossip. She could keep a secret – other people's as well as her own. But we grew closer by this reticence, becoming natural forces in each other's lives. I suppose I could accept our not interrogating each other because it came to suit me; but why it suited her I never discovered.

Other people's marriages remain a mystery to outsiders. This is often because the success of such marriages remains a mystery even to the pair involved. In the domain of bodies, appearance, blood, pheromones, genetic disposition, lies something beyond words. In Margaret's silence, I came to perceive, was something of wisdom, although it was her and not my wisdom.

So perhaps it became second nature to us. Now I think how odious the opposite situation would have been, with our every last life-incident having to be thrashed out, examined, annotated.

Reticence is not a much-lauded quality these days. Does it exaggerate to say that Margaret's reticence had a Roman quality? I came to love and respect it greatly. It was, after all, one of her qualities that stood out rock-like when the waves of illness stormed against her. Her reticence and control were relished by all who knew her – as I believe was proved by the many friends who came to her funeral.

Oh, she was important enough – even if this book would have been too emotional for her liking.

The sense of descending into a grimmer world was strong as September closed. Even the merciful Indian summer was dying. My days became choked with work. Three separate bundles of washing went into the machine and were pegged out to dry in the sun. Later, most of the clothes were ironed. During the day, I phoned here and there enquiring about a wheelchair. The Red Cross was very helpful. I also found that there was a local company, in Headington, who made stair lifts. I got an amiable man to come round and measure up our straight flight of stairs. He said it would be three weeks before the lift could be fitted.

Over the next few days, arguing that the case was urgent, I persuaded him to agree it would be fitted in two weeks. In the event, the company came through in ten days, since we were so local. It was obliging of them.

Meanwhile, what did Moggins eat on this day? I made her a tongue sandwich, cutting off the crusts. She managed to eat most of that. Her lips and mouth were so dry. I also discovered that Somerfield stocked a banana and mandarin trifle that was as tasty as a home-made one. She enjoyed that. For a while, these trifles became extremely popular with us.

She was hardly able to keep her eyes open. She dozed on the sofa until it was time to make her weary way upstairs to bed at 9 p.m.

'What a poor ruin I am!' she exclaimed, as she rested on the hall chest. I held her and cuddled her, lost for words.

The log she kept of her health was petering out. An entry for the 22nd of September – the penultimate entry – is brief:

I am as weak as a kitten in the mornings lately. Cannot do much in the way of getting up without sitting every minute to recover breath and slow heart down.

When Patti called again, Margaret confessed that she had cried a little on Patti's shoulder. (Patti said later, 'She cried to think she was leaving you alone.')

But well she might have cried,

> . . . considering the terrible disappointments dealt her by the failure of recent prescriptions to improve her state.
>
> Although life was slightly easier for her today, still she spends much time asleep, or with her eyes closed, or just sitting, trying to overcome the extreme difficulty of making the next move.
>
> Life is hell and misery and bloody boring for her. What can I do to stop it? I just want her better for a little while, to enjoy her life again until that maggot in her guts kills her. Tim and I plan to take her up to Blakeney (unspoken, 'for the last time'). If only we could get this stair lift installed. About £2,000–£2,500. Sigh.

Margaret lived under the sentence of death. The knowledge was always with her – and of course with me. Our two lives had become one life. In our earlier days, certainly, we had had our differences, some of them grave; but because we had married and made certain commitments to each other, we stayed together and resolved the differences, or let time heal them. Forgiveness is an important element in life; forgiveness is better than revenge, its opposite. Vengeance imprisons one, whereas forgiveness makes one free. We had long since forgiven one another; and, when our children left home and we were alone together, we grew extremely close – which I believe is not always the case.

So complete was my contentment with life, it salved the perilous, if temporary, dip in my literary reputation. So complete was it that, had I been religious, I would have believed God was punishing my complacency.

So congenial had our joint life become, we had not thought of its abrupt termination. We had a smaller home, which we had made quite comfortable; and, as far as we envisaged the future, we saw ourselves growing old together. I was expected to die first. It was proving extremely difficult to confront an entirely changed prospect.

I could scarcely believe the diminution of Margaret's energies. Still I foolishly hoped that a different pill would improve matters.

In my diary, I try to reason myself into acceptance of the inevitable, pointing out that we had enjoyed so many years of contentment and fun that that should fortify me; a sharper regret would have entered the picture had we been continually quarrelling.

Furthermore, I had always known, but perhaps had forgotten of recent years, that life was no sinecure. In the words of a character in one of my plays, 'No great religion ever promised life was going to be a picnic.' One might as well be courageous. Like almost anything else, courage is a habit. It's easy. One soldiers on.

It may be that my wife had come to the same conclusion.

Our lives had become frugal. That suited me well enough.

In better days, it was our custom for me to join her in the kitchen and pour us each a glass of red wine, which we drank while she prepared supper. That habit had died, along with much of the food habit. I lost my appetite,

seeing hers dwindle. I drank no alcohol in the evening.
When passing the last two hours of the day alone downstairs, I merely sipped my small glass of San Pelegrino water
with a single square of Ritter dark chocolate. There was
always San Pelegrino and Volvic in the house. And Ritter
dark chocolate.

When October dawned, we again eschewed our custom to
look at each other across the pillows and wish each other a
happy month. My prayer was that she would live through
this month.

We had decided we would go to Blakeney.

Margaret's mouth was so dry. At midday, she took some
home-made chicken soup and a yoghurt. She had difficulty
speaking.

I was beside myself with anguish. I rang Patti Pugh at
Sobell House, needing her moral support. She was elsewhere.

Margaret could scarcely get out of bed that morning. She
lay there helpless, eyes closed, head lolling against the pillow.
It had all happened so fast. I went upstairs several times to see
how she was. Always the same, unmoving.

When I took her a cup of Marmite, she roused slightly,
saying with sorrow, 'I don't know how much longer I will be
able to dress myself.' I held her hand. She sipped at the
Marmite, then set down the cup.

'I'm not sure whether I can make it to Blakeney tomorrow.'

Oh my dear love, what anguish you are in! I, too, for your
sweet sake. Your intellect is still clear. When you gaze up at
me, I read in your eyes that you know you are dying. If only I

could give my life for yours, you should gladly have it! You are
so much more needed than I, and so much the better person.

Patti rang back. She thinks the flecainide pills could be
administered at double strength. I asked if this would damage
the heart still further; she did not think so. Neil, however, said
to wait until we returned from Norfolk.

On the 2nd of October, we were in our apartment in Quay
House, Blakeney. It was a triumph of the human spirit. Tim
drove us there in the new car. Margaret felt safer that way.

I had shopped in the morning, getting cat food and
Nurishment. I bought a stunning clump of rooted golden
chrysanthemums in a pot, to thank Wendy for looking after
the cats while we were away. I rushed to the Red Cross and
rented a wheelchair from them. And I accepted Carters' esti-
mate for the installation of the new doors.

'Please get on with it!' It was a plea we had also made to
the stair-lift man, and to the publisher of Margaret's book –
the latter without result or even response.

Moggins became very cheerful when Tim arrived. As Mark
said, 'He always has a galvanising effect on Chris.' By two in
the afternoon, we were off, M in high spirits to think we were
heading for good old Norfolk again.

In the flat, Margaret could sit at one of her windows and
look out over the quayside, the cut and the marshes, with all
their subtle colours, to the distant murmuring sea. It was a
view she had painted and photographed, a view of which we
did not tire. There she was again, in the flat she had chosen
and bought independently, furnished mainly with her
mother's furniture. Tim and I cooked lamb chops for supper

and, after Margaret had gone to bed, watched that magical, sexy film *Walkabout* on TV.

The following day was a bowlful of sun and stillness. Startlingly, Margaret was up first. I woke to hear her filling the kettle for early morning tea. Had the clocks gone back a year?

We take a bath in the gigantic bath every day when we are here; it is too deep and luxurious to miss. It caused some trouble this morning. I bathed first, immersing myself in suds. Moggins followed, and found she was not strong enough to climb out.

There followed a scene of painful and grotesque humour. After suggesting we flooded the bath and floated her out ('You can swim, can't you?'), I pulled and heaved at the lady from all angles. She laughed and gasped and suffered, but could not get her legs under her.

'Oh, I must be turning into a jellyfish!'

Eventually, I had to take off my socks and trousers and climb into the bath behind her. More laughter.

Arms under armpits and – hup! – we were away! Poor girl. I know she will never venture into that bath again. In any case, it must have been designed with an Hungarian baron in mind.

We had a good day, leading the simple Norfolk life. On the modest heights above Salthouse, we admired the beautiful view and gave the Red Cross wheelchair some exercise. In West Runton, we discovered some amateur attempts to make financial capital out of the mammoth skeleton excavated from the sandy cliffs. The Post Office was selling a mammoth video. We searched for mammoth sandwiches but had to settle for crab, which we ate on the beach. Moggins seemed happy and quite well, although she preferred to stay in the back of the car. We all laughed a lot; she was glad to have Tim's pleasant company. It was a blessed interlude.

It was her idea to invite Bernard and Suzy up from the flat below. They came for a drink at 5.30 and she told them of her illness, told it straight and without self-pity. They were shocked and sympathetic, but sensible. Moggins informed them that Tim and Charlotte would inherit the flat.

It seems I still clung to the illusion that there was hope of a remission. That entry continues:

If she can't get better – if only she might stay as she is now, with me waiting on her, so that we could all share her presence, her counsel, her laughter . . . At times, at many times, I cannot believe she is going to get worse. The slightest remission and I hope again – as perhaps she does.

Bernard said to her, 'But you'll keep coming up here?'

'Oh yes, of course,' she said. Yet I think we both realise that she is saying goodbye to this haven of hers. Oh, it breaks your heart. How can we – how can we possibly bear it?

On the Saturday, we drove over to Holt to call on Betty and Antony in their recently acquired bungalow. It was Tim's first visit there. Betty has it beautifully decorated in her best Victorian style. They were very sad about Margaret's illness, of course; but like the rest of the family they acted cheerful. They led us to the hamlet of West Beckham, and a grand pub called The Wheatsheaf, a pretty brick building set in agreeable dishevelled grounds.

We wheeled Margaret in in her wheelchair. The landlord

came forward and was genial and helpful, steering us to a pleasant table, where we ate lunch. Margaret only pecked at something, but in that affliction she had company, since Antony also struggled with his food.

Back at the flat, Tim and I helped her up the stairs. Her eyes gleamed so brightly when I kissed her goodnight. Her slender arms went about my neck. She exclaimed what a happy break this short excursion was.

On the way home, we stopped for some lunch at the Fakenham Safeway. Margaret did not want to leave the car. We parked it so that Tim and I could see her as we sat over a disgusting coffee in the coffee bar. There she was, beloved wife and mother, not moving, frail and quiet, so changed from her former bright self.

Tim is very steady. We talked man-to-man. He had a problem: could he bring forward the date of his wedding to Sarah? It was not possible to unscramble arrangements already made, but how about some preliminary form of ceremony in the local church? No one knew how much longer she had, so I couldn't say.

We talked about the funeral. It was the first time I had dared discuss this matter with anyone. How do you go about arranging such matters? He couldn't say.

As soon as we arrived home, Wendy, Mark and Thomas appeared, all cheery, just as the men on Captain Scott's Antarctic expedition put a brave face on things, even to the last white-out. We had tea together, chatting and joking, much as we had always done.

That evening, Gary and Dede called from Chicago. They had some news. They had just learned that Chicago

University's School of Medicine was developing an experimental drug, so far known as Onyx-015, designed to kill cancerous tumours. One section of the research was concentrating on pancreatic cancers that had spread to the liver. Gary impressed on me that this project was only at Phase One; but the School of Medicine was inviting volunteers to attend their clinics.

I became excited. Hope burned again.

Margaret was upstairs, preparing for bed. I went up and explained to her the possibility of flying to Chicago for the tests. Of course I would be there with her.

She listened before replying simply, 'I couldn't do it.'

Gary faxed me a two-page letter concerning the treatment proposed. It emphasised that Phase One meant the drug had been tested only on animals so far. I faxed copies of the letter to Mark, who works at the Cochrane Collaboration, an international charity that systematically reviews randomised controlled trials of the effects of health care. Mark's work is to coordinate the search for random and controlled trials of cancer. I also faxed Gary's letter to Neil, to greet him in the morning.

Anything, *anything*, that might prolong my sweet wife's life is worth trying.

After much silence from upstairs, I go to see how she is. She sits at the modest little desk that she has always used as her dressing table. An almost unopened bottle of her favourite perfume, Blue Grass, stands there. Her eyes are closed. So I help her get her trousers and panties off. I undress her completely and slip her nightdress on.

She gasps. 'I seem to be extra tired this evening.'

I kiss her, hold her, fondle her. How cold her face is.

I was unable to sleep. I kept visualising us in first class on a Boeing 747, flying in to Chicago O'Hare, me looking after her, keeping up the supplies of mineral water. Gary and Dede meeting us at the airport, and driving us straight to the hospital. All arrangements going smoothly. A course of injections. Margaret rejuvenated. Perhaps it was not too late, even now. Even now. Pray it was not too late.

I heaved myself out of bed. At 8.15, I was at the shops, buying a loaf of bread for breakfast. Despite myself, I could not help enjoying the fine morning. Despite myself, my spirits rose. We could save her.

And I parked my new 850 in the car park with a line of other cars. Distance-locking was still a novelty. I tried pressing the zapper to discover over what distance it would work. What fun! How many other car doors might it accidentally unlock?

This was a scene from a musical . . . Gene Kelly comes dancing out of Somerfield into the car park. A variety of cars are lined up, silent and empty. Gene flashes his zapper. All the cars light up. All their doors fly open, right down the line, one after the other. '*I'm singin' and dancin' in the car park . . .*'

But this turns out to be a very bad day for her. Far from getting to Chicago, going to Blakeney has exhausted her. It seemed she wanted nothing, sipping at mineral water, eating no breakfast. Eyes closed.

I did a load of washing and ironed most of it during the day. Since Moggins no longer came into the kitchen, I kept the ironing board up and pans piled on top of the oven for easy access.

She wanted no lunch, only Nurishment. No one phoned. Nothing from Neil. Silence. It was early afternoon before she managed to get herself downstairs. She sprawled on the sofa, eyes closed. Very depressed. She did not complain, simply murmuring that she was tired.

I phoned Charlotte. She sounded very reserved.

That night, I lay awake beside my wife, listening to her rapid little mouse breaths.

We had to return to the JR to learn the results of the ECG. This entailed the rigmarole of the Red Cross wheelchair. It was very heavy and difficult to lift into the back of the Volvo. However, it was easier to use in the hospital than were their own recalcitrant chairs. So we sailed through the JR, from one department to another.

Margaret had a chest X-ray and an echo scan. We were mainly under the neat Dr Hart. He is kind and friendly, and answers our questions; but he can produce no cardiological miracle cures.

While Margaret was on the couch being scanned, I was able to watch the reading on a monitor. In various shades of grey, her beating heart seemed to grow a gulping mouth, gulping, gasping, gasping. The operator faded in electrical impulses. Now, electric storms, yellow, red and blue, much as you might expect to see on the face of Jupiter, raged over the face of her gulping heart. I was aghast, fearing for the worst. It looked to me like a disaster, but Dr Hart was cheerful.

'It's very good. The heart is quite normal.'

'Apart from . . . ?'

Admittedly, the heart beat from the centre, not from the top, so that less blood got pumped. But the amount pumped would be perfectly adequate when M was sitting still. Only when challenged by activity would the supply prove inadequate.

Maybe, Dr Hart supposed, the flecainide could be changed for another similar drug. And the diuretic should be discontinued. He would speak to Neil MacLennan.

We thanked him. He courteously held the door open for the wheelchair to pass. We went home to wait.

No good news awaited us. Gary phoned to say that the section of the Onyx research dealing with drugs for the pancreas and liver is not in Chicago but San Francisco. Our supportive friends in Chicago had made that city seem close. But San Francisco sounded very far away. I realised that Moggins could never make it.

Mark rang with a long and careful exposition of what the research entails. One would not have known that he was at a crisis point in his and Wendy's joint life. Onyx is a big pharmaceutical company. Phase One means that the drug is in a very early stage. No commitment is made about its efficacy. And, indeed, it will be tested on patients, a percentage of whom will receive a placebo.

Nevertheless, the company had received ten thousand (I forget the actual figure) volunteers. Those volunteers would have to stay in a clinic for some months, under observation.

In the nature of things, the company would want young and otherwise healthy patients. Ladies over sixty with heart problems are unlikely bets, and would threaten the improvement rate.

Besides which, it will be easier to take volunteers from local populations.

Best to forget the idea. And the hope it brought.

So fear again, fear and sorrow.

It's now 10.50 p.m. Margaret is still washing. She is always scrupulously clean. She went upstairs about half an hour ago. Dragged herself up. It's a great labour for her. Everything seems like a great labour.

Don't leave me, my darling! I'm afraid. What can life be without you, your humour, your warmth, your dear womanly kindness?

Other dramas close to home were in process. On Wednesday the 8th of October, Mark phoned at 8.30 to say that Wendy and he had gone to the hospital at four in the morning. Wendy had had an epidural and her waters had broken. She was in good spirits.

I burst into tears at the news. Margaret and I huddled together in the bedroom, crying convulsively.

At noon, I went round to the hospital. Wendy lay there, sizeable but bright, snug in her dimly lit room, with two perky young midwives in attendance. They seemed to be having a great time. Contractions had started.

When Mark rang again, jubilantly, the baby had been born! A beautiful boy of 9lbs 10.5ozs, with a thatch of dark hair. Wendy was absolutely fine.

At 5.30, I manoeuvred brave Chris into the wheelchair and we chugged round to the hospital to visit mother and child. The marvellous babe snoozed peacefully. Wendy looked radiant. We took some photos.

I was madly proud of my dear daughter; she has borne herself and her baby so bravely, so stylishly. And of Mark too – a good caring man, who went to the trouble of researching the Onyx situation even as the hour of crisis approached.

We rang Clive and also Bet and Ant, and generally rejoiced. The great chain of Being: a new life, new hope.

Thursday 9th October

Wendy phoned early. At 12.15 I was round with her and her still nameless little boy. I regard the tiny mite with reverence. It is so calm after one of life's most strenuous adventures. Wendy is energetic and cheerful. Mark arrives, looking a little pale.

I was meant to drive them home. In the end, I drove them nowhere but round the hospital grounds, since the hospital wanted an X-ray of an enlarged kidney from which we knew the babe suffered. I brought most of Wendy's kit round here; they were going home by taxi. I returned in time to give Margaret a little lunch.

Mark called to collect Wendy's things. He is off to Amsterdam for a conference tomorrow. I am off to London in an hour. A weaving lady, Janet Phillips, very neat, is with Margaret.

My visit to London was simply to attend a reception at the Reform Club for the launch of Peter Kemp's *Oxford Companion to Literary Quotations*. Four Aldiss quotations are included in the volume. A fairly dull party. A lady gave a short speech with her eyes closed. I bummed a ciggy off Deborah Moggach's charming daughter.

On the day following, engineers arrived at Hambleden smartly at nine to install the stair lift. They juggled the main bar in through the bathroom window. By four in the afternoon, the lift was complete and ready for action.

I tested it out. Margaret tested it out. It worked.

Margaret ascended grandly, giving me a regal wave as she went.

The cats had yet to try it, although it was a great success with Thomas when he came round to experiment. He's so bright. He swiftly mastered the controls, shouting with laughter as he did so.

It was as well that Margaret felt a little better, since we received several visitors, apart from the technicians.

Patti came, and Father Michael, the local vicar, who offered us Holy Communion in the house. He's a clever and good-humoured man, but we have to stick to our lack of principles. I admired him and made him a mug of tea. Later, Neil came. He got wine.

At this time came Margaret's final entry in the computer log of her health. She had become too exhausted to write more.

Monday 13th October
   All doctors mucking about with pills: had a twenty-four-hour ECG scan fitted to me, which showed high pulse rate, so went to see Dr Hart again and had proper scan and chest X-ray. All pretty good, though heart beating only 'from the middle downwards'.

> *Put me on flecainide. Very nasty results, very feeble,*
> *legs unsteady. After two weeks came off it.*
>   *Now trying many fewer pills, no diuretics.*
>   *Brian has immediately got a stair lift fitted! Brilliant,*
> *life much easier! We also have a wheelchair. I eat very*
> *little at present, drink mostly. But biggest news of all:*
> *WENDY'S BABY ARRIVED ON 8TH OCTOBER,*
> *1.40 p.m. A dear little creature. B wheeled me in to see*
> *them at 6 p.m.!*

And with that happy note, her entries cease for ever . . .

A merciful respite. Moggins seemed well in control. I drove to see the new baby in Bainton Road. Since Mark was away, his sister Sharon, dark-haired, round-eyed, was standing in for him.

When I arrived, Wendy was sitting in the kitchen on a hard-backed chair, smiling contentedly, with the baby on her lap. She looked so good, so beautiful – I'd even say full of power: the very image of motherhood. Sharon gave me a coffee. Thomas was there, cheerful and well behaved. Together we unwrapped Clive and Youla's present for Young Sausage, a bedroom lamp with a pretty revolving shade, and Margaret's and my present, a rug with Noah's Ark animals on.

In the evening, Sharon had to go home. Kindly Auntie Chagie took over, bathing Thomas. She was going to cook lunch the next day, the Sunday. Margaret felt able to suggest we might go.

Margaret seemed less assailed; now was the reign of King

Veramapil, King Flecainide being deposed. We had no visitors in the afternoon, which pleased her. She sat in the living-room while I baked my first cake.

She ate a little supper, perhaps to please me, and was fine and cheerful. Moggins, my darling, I still keep thinking you will get better – it's terrible! I can't help it! That radiant smile of yours is so life-enhancing.

At least your pretty feet are better, now you are off them so much. They are so tender and youthful. I nurse and kiss them.

Thieves came that night and dug up and stole our little rowan tree, which Margaret had planted in the drive. It was loaded with berries. To steal a tree is the height of scoundrelly meanness.

No doubt it was sold next morning at a car boot sale.

I took Margaret in the wheelchair just from our back door to the car, a matter merely of fifteen yards. Then off to Wendy's.

Moggins is always with me, and I with her. How I shall miss her – oh, I still can't bear to think of it. You'd never in a million years find a lady of such delicate sensibilities.

At Wendy's, there was some delay, since Chagie lacked basmati rice for lunch. Owen saved the day by arriving with a packet. We ate a chicken risotto in the pleasant rear room.

Only Thomas was not present. I had been reading to him from Henri Troyat's *Life of Pushkin*. Unfortunately, he had fallen asleep during a chapter about cholera in the village of Borodono.

Once we were home again, both Moggins and I fell asleep. I woke an hour later, cold, my blood turned to jelly. She was in pretty good fettle, all things considered.

We were amused by a programme on BBC Radio 3, a documentary about an old friend, dead by some years, Kyril Bonfiglioli, author of a clutch of comic novels. His widow, Margaret Bon, and Maggie Noach, Hilary Rubinstein and I, and other friends, talked about his idiosyncratic character. Many of the more ribald anecdotes were left out, but still it was a funny programme.

Margaret and I had a discussion later about her illness.

'Sometimes I wish all my troubles would fly away,' she said. How typical of her, that moderating 'sometimes'. And my heart breaks once more . . .

We hold each other on the bed, embracing, kissing, whispering sweet endearments.

Now I sit alone, not reading, not watching TV. Yet knowing I am not alone: she is upstairs, alive, sensitive, sensible. I'll see her again soon.

Next Saturday, the Cassini-Huygens probe begins its long journey – past Jupiter in January 2000, past Saturn in 2004, when, a billion miles from Earth, it will launch a probe into Titan's atmosphere. I caught myself hoping I might be alive to witness the results. Titan, that pre-biotic satellite, tickles the imagination.

[VII]

The days of sad October slipped by. The leaves of trees took on hectic colour and blew away. Still we lived together, unaware that Margaret had entered the final month of her life. I suppose there were telltale signs, for those practised in the detection of such matters.

Perhaps we had lived too soon. New methods of treating cancer are being developed, with antibody-directed enzymes, and so on. In another ten years, many forms of cancer will be curable.

And yet Margaret was experiencing an hitherto unknown variety of caring. Much expertise went into her case, if only to retreat baffled. A more holistic approach had grown, which saw in cancerous illness a disruption of the lives of the family and not simply of the patient; this followed the tearing away of the secrecy (always a companion to fear) that had previously surrounded cancer. The introduction of Macmillan nurses acknowledged the link between medicine and spiritual suffering: another holistic advance. Hospices are another sign of greatly improved understanding of illness, and of spiritual health in the face of death.

Western medicine has come in for much criticism, some of it no doubt deserved. However, its positive side must be acknowledged, and its willingness to advance, abandoning old received attitudes as it goes.

It might be asked, why did we not try unorthodox fringe

medical cures – what you might call madical cures? The answer was simple. Neither of us had any faith in them.

Perhaps we were too close to the situation to observe the steady downward trend in Margaret's condition. Occasionally, though, the truth peered out like a grinning skull, as for instance when I drove her to Sobell House one afternoon.

It was our second visit to the hospice. Once more we entered by the automatic glass doors, turned right, and went along the winding passage to the doctors' quarters. On the previous occasion, Margaret had walked there; on this occasion, I pushed her in the wheelchair.

We saw Dr Michael Minton, a kindly man, perhaps. He examined Margaret and took a sample of blood. It now seems her blood pressure is low (150/75) – after months, years, of her being troubled by high blood pressure.

I suppose it's fairly obvious that time is running out – obvious even to my brave wife, who cried a little at one point; and although this whole notebook is about time running out, still I can't credit it whenever I clutch her, when I stroke her hair and kiss her cheeks and lips.

With Dr Minton, we went over Margaret's case history once again. Until 7th August, when she had the laparoscopy in the Acland, she was walking about as usual; she certainly had her problems, but she also had her strength. Ever since that date, it has been a struggle for her. Try as she may, she gets weaker.

It seems the one prescription that has had a positive effect is the mouth spray, Luborin, which Neil prescribed for her dry mouth. Otherwise, there's no evidence that anything else they have tried has helped her, although certainly the steroids produced some colour in her cheeks. Poor darling, she does realise how fatal everything is.

It is hard, I find, not to feel antagonism towards medicos when they appear so helpless. I'm so desperate I could not help radiating hostility. I kept quiet, but felt myself about to achieve critical mass.

When Minton took a blood sample from Margaret, I thought of the quacks of the eighteenth century, bleeding their patients. Maybe we should hire a witchdoctor. I simply cannot bear for her to die. The better half of my life – far more than that – will die with her. Let it die! Let me too wither and die.

Best of a bad day was when Jon Stallworthy arrived with a lovely chicken pie Jill had baked. We ate a quarter of it for supper – or rather, I did.

The Booker Prize has been won by Arundhati Roy's *The God of Small Things*. Moggins read and enjoyed it, although not without the occasional squeak at its over-ornate style.

My notes continue, becoming the diary of a self-torturer. Blood on the sheets.

Wednesday 15th October

Another dull day, and a bad start to it. Moggins reported her excreta was reddy-orange in hue. Was there blood in it?

She rests. As ever she rests. I have to try to get some work done. Tim arrives some time today. That will cheer her up.

I look with despair into her kitchen cupboards. Here lie items once part of a serene going concern, never to be used again: stem ginger, dried basil, poppadums, grated Parmesan in packet, carmenncita (whatever that is), whole nutmegs, *lingots blancs*, Tullamore dew, blends of wild and cultivated rices, black eye beans, tartaric acid in powder form, etc.

On the back of the kitchen cupboard door hangs Moggins's smart navy-blue blazer jacket. She will never wear it again.

This time, I've got it firmly into my head.

This is a low day, a sad day, a bad day. We face our awful situation – which has to be faced over and over again. She cries on my shoulder in bed. How can I comfort her?

The liver has enlarged, so that she can scarcely eat. The dull ache about her middle creeps onwards, steadily increasing. She finally comes downstairs on the stair lift, laughs at her frailty.

I assist her to the study. There she sits and directs the filing of documents. Everything is orderly. I feel the strangeness of this relationship.

We give way to the misery she has fought for so long. We hold each other and burst out crying, two heavy showers of tears.

'It has come on so fast,' she sobs.

'Try to live with us as long as you can.'

'I love you so much.'

'What will it be like in the house when you are gone? I might as well be on Mars.'

Many tears, many tissues. We are the benefactors of flower shops and Kleenex.

We feel no better after the storm, realising what misery we're in. I vacuum the living-room carpet with the Dyson, to which I have never taken. She moves to the living-room for a rest, clutching the walls as she goes. I vacuum the study carpet in order to smarten up for Tim's coming. He will cheer her a little.

He arrives in the mighty DRU, in time for lunch. He hugs his mum. She bursts into tears.

For lunch, she has soup only. Tim and I eat some paté.

Our nice Macmillan nurse Patti calls. So does the gardener. I really have no mind for him, but potter about and talk out of politeness. Smartly dressed Patti finds us at a low point. Her mode of consolation is what we need: grim, but humorous. She permits, even encourages, desolation. She perceives that for us it wards off despair. Educational for Tim.

Tim is to stay over-night. I rush out and collect a video I had ordered, *Eat Drink Man Woman*, the Taiwanese film directed by Ang Lee. Margaret and I had laughed so much over this film. She wanted to see the astonishing opening sequence again. She did see it, and then she went upstairs to bed.

Doing the washing up, I realised I must wash the tea towels tomorrow. A bit of an eye-opener, really. One towel is plain, one floral, one exhibits Shakespeare's head, one carries views of Fakenham, one has a logo in the corner: *Le Vrai Gourmet*. No gourmets here: this has become Starvation Corner. I am still surprised by the number of things that require regular washing.

Thursday 16th October

The delayed Cassini probe has lifted off for Jupiter and Saturn. The British car, Thrust, has broken the land-speed record. I love these male nouns, probe, thrust . . .

Margaret's sense of delicacy. She will say to strangers on the phone, 'I'm not too well at present.' I'd be screaming, 'I'm dying, you bastards!'

I woke rather late, at 8.15, and got up immediately.
Margaret was still sleeping, looking peaceful. Tim also asleep. I
came downstairs, fed the cats, and prepared Margaret's
breakfast, which is easily done. It now consists of one slice of
Ryvita with butter and honey, a glass of milk, and a mug of
camomile and honey tea (which smells delightful and reminds
us of happy Jug days).

I was forced to scud off into town, to return our smart but
too heavy wheelchair to the Red Cross in the Banbury Road.
Strange, interesting people in the depot. Then a half-hour with
Wendy, who is peaceful and happy, alone with her lovely baby.
A tonic to be with her undisturbed and hear all her news. Clive
has sent some excellent photos of our happy al fresco meal on
my birthday, with Chris looking good.

Wendy remarked on how really beautiful Chris looked when
we lunched with her in Bainton Road, the Sunday before last.

After lunch, I had to go to the Urology Clinic in the
Churchill. It was an appointment of long standing. Dr Ho and a
student mucked me about and asked questions. Passing blood
two years ago has told against me. They sussed out the cyst on
my right kidney and discovered a wart on my left testicle. I
have to return some day and have my bladder enquired into.

'Please don't bother,' I said. 'I don't care.'

Moggins was sitting downstairs when I got home, a bit sad
that Tim had left to return to work. In no time, in trooped
Vanessa and Roger, proud possessors of Woodlands. I don't
know what they thought of this hovel, although they were
complimentary. Funnily, we chatted like old friends. This world
my love is forced to leave is full of amazing people. Moggins
looked lovely in her new orange slacks. Roger and I arranged

to give our agents lunch in Michel's and draw up a contract for *White Mars.*

They talked freely about Woodlands and its gardens. Margaret surely felt as I did, a great yearning for our simple happy years there.

Then Neil turned up over what we laughingly call supper. Cancer is good for social life. He examined Margaret. Her blood pressure is now 125/70, which apparently represents an improvement over Tuesday's reading, perhaps because she's now ceased taking several of her useless drugs.

Neil and family are off to the South of France on Saturday. I saw him out to his car.

'You can forget about all your lousy patients for a few days.'

'I'm very fond of my nice patients,' he said. A cheerful man. Not too cheerful, thank God!

Mornings were increasingly bad for Margaret; she found it difficult to waken fully. Two days later, and her breakfast had dwindled still further, to a slice of Ryvita and a glass of milk.

So these banal domesic details were played out in the face of eternity. When you grow old, details become your only defence.

When she did manage to get washed and dressed, a new wheelchair arrived. I settled her into it and, with great exertion, managed to push her up the ramp on to the lawn, and so finally to inspect our new flowerbed, newly weeded, in which the red dahlias still flourished.

It now seems strange that until this time I had had no assistance with Margaret. Enter Monique, the district nurse – quite a cutie, and not at all my antiquated idea of a district nurse.

She stayed a while, talking and being sweet to Margaret. She could have stayed all night for my money. Margaret seemed cheered too, and there was talk of an oxygen cylinder becoming available, and of a physiotherapist.

And even at this rather desperate time, there were still intermissions of brightness. Since the day was so beautiful and serene, I helped Margaret into the car, loaded in the wheelchair, and off we went – 'for a spin', as our parents used to say. We headed for Woodstock but, as we were going through Begbroke, we suddenly decided we would look at one of our old homes, Orchard House.

We stopped by the church and were gazing on the alterations to the old eighteenth-century mansion when its owner came out to see who was there. I called to him from the car, apologising for our curiosity, and explaining we had once lived here.

The man was immediately friendly. After a chat, he invited us in to look at the alterations that had been carried out since we had left in 1982. His name was Nicholas. He was French and an airline pilot.

As we were escorted round, Margaret in her wheelchair, sundry children appeared, all very polite, and then Nicholas's wife, Deborah, an attractive lady with china-doll blue eyes and a baby at the breast. Somehow we were immediately friendly. While Margaret talked to Deborah, Nicholas showed me round the grounds. He had planted a copse in the field.

Both house and garden looked beautiful in the autumn sun. I'm at a loss to explain the extreme happiness that filled us. It must have emanated from Nicholas and Deborah and their children.

'We think it's a paradise for the children,' Deborah said.

But every ointment has its fly. Nicholas worried, just as we had, about the cost of upkeep. He had not heated the beautiful well-situated swimming pool, in which our children had become semi-aquatic all one long summer, years ago. And I recalled a time when Charlotte and I, and her friend Emma, had swum early in the year, taking advantage of a brilliant day. I had not even skimmed the pool then, and an ornamental almond tree was scattering its pink petals across the water. As we swam through them, more petals flew down on the surface, so that we emerged plastered in them.

We sat outside the conservatory and ate tea in the garden with Nicholas and Deborah. Tallulah, the eldest daughter, had baked a cake, slices of which we enjoyed. We stayed for a couple of hours, basking in friendship and happiness. Margaret was fine.

With one of my now frequent mood swings, I thought we had found the nicest people in the world. And I feared for the fragility – as I saw it – of their contentment.

It happened that we had among our pictures a pencil sketch of Orchard House, mounted but never framed. We determined to present it to the current owners. A week after our first visit, we drove back there. The front door stood ajar. I knocked; no answer came. I had to walk in. Deborah appeared, and I presented her with the sketch.

She was reminded that she had a letter for me somewhere. After some searching in a pile of old correspondence, she came on it. When I opened it later, I discovered it was from the Royal Festival Hall, asking me to confirm that I would give a reading on a date in February next. Where they had dug up this old address, who knows. It seemed that it was just as well I had called.

Deborah came out and spoke to Margaret, who was sitting placidly in the car. She exclaimed how fond of us she had become. Later, at the funeral – did we but know it, such a short time away – she produced two photographs I treasure, of us with Margaret looking her old self, sitting at their tea-table . . .

We drove home. Margaret on that occasion was exhausted. She staggered into the house and collapsed on the sofa.

My diary remarks that it is hard to despair when there are such good and trusting people about. Later, however, I found it tolerably easy. This despite a visit from Sue Brack; phone calls to Hilary, taking on a new lease of life since his hip replacement; and Petronilla, whose spine had been cracked in hospital, and who was having a bad time all round. Suddenly, everyone had their troubles.

Joan and Harry Harrison called, laughing and jovial. They were thinking of moving to Brighton, to be near their daughter Moira. They were also contemplating a villa in Lugano, which city, according to Harry, has 'Italian cooking, Swiss telephone system'.

In any case, they were off in December to Mexico and California, to over-winter for three months.

To cheer me as they left, Joan said, 'My mother had exactly Margaret's trouble. She lived five years, Brian – five years!'

This news I received like a blow.

I cannot possibly continue to work as I am doing now.
However much I long for Margaret to live – to be well again

and not forever under the shadow – five years of this slow-
burning crisis would probably kill us both.

The misery had been reinforced that morning by Margaret's decision to take a bath. She enjoyed her soak and then found, as in Blakeney, she could not get out, although the bath here is much shallower. She now weighed only nine stone. Yet I could not lift her, try as I might. Eventually, as in Blakeney, I had to kick off my shoes, socks and trousers and climb in the bath behind her. I heaved from that position. Laughs, groans, gasps! The poor lady then managed to turn towards me for support and get to her knees. I helped her dry herself.

It was a bad adventure for her. We were both exhausted.

Am I right in thinking that everything in the house is going to hell in a handcart? Nothing's as clean as once it was – or in the correct place. The business side of things – well, it's in collapse. Margaret can't even write thank you notes. She no longer opens up the Performa to see what e-mail is there.

As for my literary ambitions, I now despise them. They were an illusion. While the *TLS* and the *New Scientist* still arrive here regularly, I can hardly bring myself to look at them. All that side of life is finished.

At one time – an age ago – two weeks? – there was a terrible waste of food here. Everything got thrown out. Nowadays, I have pretty well given up shopping. I buy mineral water and loaves of bread. Bread and water. Oh, and plebeian packet soup. She likes packet soup if I strain away the croutons and bits and pieces. I always add sherry to her

soup – a good Scottish habit I picked up from her, although
she worries it may affect her liver . . .

She has a talent to accept, to make no comment about her
being unable to eat solid things. She lies with her knees up, on
the sofa, or in bed. She is inclined to mumble. It's so cruel, so
cruel. Betty's a great help. I can phone her and talk frankly to her.

If I seem to complain here – why, it's nothing, nothing.
She's still living, still with me, her dear self. Of course I love
her – she gives my life and all I do reason. The books I
wrote . . . Don't let her die. Yet, yet day by day she does die,
slipping just an inch nearer the brink.

That this should happen to her . . .

As for that inch nearer . . . The days were drawing in. The
weather became colder, the skies duller.

Another week began. I went shopping as quickly as possible, for cat food and little else, while Margaret half-ate her
breakfast. She had her usual trouble with beginning the day.
She sat in bed, eyes closed, pillows behind her. The trouble
with the bed was that she kept slipping down it. I had to haul
her up again, which was surely painful for her.

She told me she could not dress herself much longer.

'I will stay in bed today, and rest.'

'Won't it be too boring for you?'

She did not answer, simply closed her eyes.

Later on, she did get up, because David and Edith Holt
were coming in the afternoon. We slept after what we still
called lunch. Macramé came and slept on my hip, purring
me to sleep. On wakening, I found my blood had turned to
jelly as usual.

Margaret actually tottered through into the study, wearing her smart apricot slacks. She did a little work on the VAT bills but made many errors with the printing out. She looked so patiently and resignedly at me, never became angry; but oh, the pain for us both in seeing her precious life forces drain away.

Hardly had the Holts gone when our good-natured vicar, Father Michael, called and left us some home-made plum jam.

Gallant Trish Simms phoned. She was now fighting Margaret's battle to have her Boars Hill anthology published, and to get her tardy publisher off the button. Once I worried greatly that her book would not appear in time, but now it seems Margaret had simply lost all interest. She has just let it go, as she had to relinquish the hope of seeing Tim married in the spring. As she has had to let many things go, and draw in upon herself.

I was watching a young and sprightly woman age in a matter of weeks and become old.

Her I idolised. There never had been and would never be again such a perfect woman for me. True, she was reserved (though not as reserved as outsiders might think), but that could be ascribed to her having been an only child, which she always regretted. I liked her the way she was. However, I found that this admiration was not entirely reciprocated.

While having to look in her desk for some share certificates, I came across Margaret's diaries, chubby books with page-a-day entries. I found I was much criticised. It was painful for her to live with what she called 'a celebrity'. At a party I 'held court'. I was a workaholic. I was nice to her in private but in public ignored her. I had 'failed dismally' to grow vegetables in the Woodlands garden. I seemed interested 'in nothing but his bloody work'. I'm a rotten driver. I drank too much.

The diaries afford me instruction in many faults I was scarcely aware I had. Turning the pages, I failed to find a positive word about me – although I did once give 'a good little talk' in Watford Public Library . . .

So all in all, my poor dear lady had been very much less content with me than I with her. I have read in the newspapers that such is frequently the case in marriages. It is extremely sad – humiliating, in fact. The diaries were not concealed; it was intended I read them.

After much sorrowful thought, I consoled myself, as I had done previously, with an old French saying, 'In every love affair there is one who kisses and one who turns the cheek.' And yet . . . of course she had loved me, had loved and cared for me, had loved me when the fifties were turning into the sixties, when there was precious little to be gained by loving me. My first marriage had broken down. I was living in one room in the old Paradise Square – itself rather broken down. Mine was a run-down bohemian life. A profile in the *Guardian* described me as 'raffish'. She loved me *then*! But I was the man who stood by her during a long and unpleasant illness, and who loved and cared for her in sickness and in health.

Margaret's diaries make it clear indirectly what a good manager and business woman she was. How much more able she would have been at living on alone, rather than I!

She was by no means a cold person. Although I took the first step to advance our friendship in our *Oxford Mail* days, I had reason to behave with decorum. Margaret was the first to make direct sexual advances, by inviting me to her Titty Dance. Ah, the famous Titty Dance!

In those days, she shared a flat in a house, number 82, on the Banbury Road, with her friend Kay. It was spacious and comfortable. On the evening of the Titty Dance, Kay was away. Margaret removed her blouse and her brassière, revealing her shapely bosom, and commenced the dance. It was beautiful and enticing, and enough to lure on any male onlooker. She gently moved her arms and her breasts swayed forward and then back, so that sometimes her pale armpits were revealed, sometimes not. She hummed as she did so. A secret smile stole over her face. She was well aware of the effect she was having. It was irresistibly erotic.

When the dance ended, I grabbed hold of her, kissed and licked those pretty breasts, and tried to discover what else she had to offer, what hidden excitements lay under her kilted skirt. As if she could not have foreseen this move, she struggled to detain me, as my hands went first this way and that. We rolled together on the carpet. Finally, I reached the Promised Land.

When my hand was on it, she ceased struggling. I picked her up bodily and carried her into the bedroom.

So who seduced whom? Now she has gone, I am tormented by phantasms of her perfect nakedness, and that lively body.

Many matters needed attention. The second sofa ordered long ago had not arrived. The new doors had not been fitted. Nor had I heard about *Twinkling*. There was the shameful business of delay on Margaret's book.

Tim and Sarah came, and stayed overnight. On the 21st of October, we had our first district nurse in action. Margaret was dressed and slowly brushing her hair when the nurse arrived. Her resistance to being washed and dressed had disappeared. She told the nurse quite eagerly that she would enjoy a bed-bath. It was agreed she should have one on Thursday.

Eventually the time came when she said, in her undramatic way, 'I think I'll have a day in bed.' And there she lay, propped up against the pillows, eyes closed for much of the time. I sat close with her, holding her cool hand, and gazing at her with compassion and sorrow.

She wept and I wept with her. Oh, alas, alas, can nothing save this flower of women?

Wendy drove over with her baby while Tim and Sarah were still with us. We all sat round Margaret's bed, admiring the infant, cuddling him, while the bedroom was filled with golden afternoon sun.

Now I had to fulfil another commitment made months earlier, when all had seemed well. Through the Turkmenistan connection, I had agreed to read my versification of some of Makhtumkuli's poems at Waterstone's bookshop in Reading.

Before I left home, I prepared my darling a Thermos flask full of strained soup, a tiny Marmite sandwich (crusts removed) and a yoghurt. She expressed herself perfectly content with this arrangement, and wanted no one to come in to be with her while I was away.

The readings went well. A genial man of mixed Armenian,

Caribbean and Turkish blood, played the guitar. We had met before, and formed a mutual liking. He plays his own compositions. One of the audience came up afterwards and thanked me touchingly for 'my most moving reading of my beautiful poems'. It is the sort of praise that makes such excursions worthwhile.

Also there was a smart young woman to whom Youssef introduced me. She had come from Ashkhabad and was attractively dressed for winter, much as the Swedes used to dress in the fifties, with copious deployment of fur. Her father is Russian, her mother Turkmen. She now lives and studies in London.

> Back here, rather anxiously, to find Margaret asleep and Radio 4 talking to itself.
>   As usual, in the night we could not sleep for a couple of hours on end.

Over and over, in my hours of solitude, I thought about her diaries and her discontent with me and my behaviour. Had I really been that bad? She had written somewhere a warning that she was 'only letting off steam'. Why had she not spoken up? It's true that writing was my obsession, my possession – that it possessed me. Other matters I could perhaps have changed, had I known they irked her. But the writing . . . well, without making excuses, it was that which allowed us to live as comfortably as we had done.

But she had said nothing, and had made our eleven years at Woodlands into the happiest of my – of our joint – life. Naturally, it hurts to think that she was less happy that I believed. But she loved me for all my faults; hers was a loving nature.

Her kindly instructions on her computer conclude with the farewell words,

> *I love you, my beloved husband, and thank you with all my heart for the loving care you are giving me at the moment (and always)?*

Thursday, 23rd October

'If my love could cure you, you'd be better tomorrow!' – The words burst from me as I see her sail up to bed on the stair lift.

'Oh, I know it, I know it', she says, looking at me with lost eyes. She still lives. I tell her again how much the whole family loves her.

Goodness knows how it was for her, but mine was a bad day. I talk so much about myself, so little about her, which was not what I set out to do. But hers are ghost days.

Besides, old habits die hard . . .

I had to take the 850 in for a service. Getting across town, to the Volvo HQ on the Botley Road and back, took up most of the day. It was a full half-hour on the bus either way. And as soon as I arrived in Motorworld, my nose started to bleed. I never have nose-bleeds. It's ridiculous!

At home, I made another jelly, my second attempt and successful this time. Margaret ate a little of the jelly for supper. She was more lively today, following her day in bed.

District Nurse Sarah had visited while I was at Motorworld, and had given her the promised bed-bath. When I returned,

Monique was present. This petite little lady could cheer anyone's day. As I escorted her from the premises, she talked quite freely. She has seen so many cancer cases . . . Regarding me quite smilingly, she said, 'People are surprising. Margaret may last until Christmas – even longer.'

We were standing by her car in our driveway. A moment of terror – of sheer rigid terror – seized me. *So it's really going to happen . . . Soon . . .*

A long while going back to Motorworld on the bus. People silent, even glum. But I've found that if you can get into conversation, particularly if you can draw in more than one person, then they become lively and friendly. Of course, it helps if one of them happens to be American.

I returned in the car to find Meeuws and Trish here. Trish is a great help to Margaret, yet even she seems unable to get Meeuws moving on the Boars Hill book. What the man is doing I have no idea.

They left and our faithful neighbour John Stanton came round from next door.

That evening, I wrote to Neil – a letter to await his return from holiday.

Today she has been up for the afternoon as usual, and quite active, seeing her publisher and an assistant, and also our neighbour. But Monique feels she may be giving up the unequal struggle.

'She needs some more domperidone. Perhaps her drug anthology needs a re-think. No doctor so far has asked to see her walk. I witness her labours every day. I know she'll be

happy to have you visit again – although as ever she never
states her desires. Of course, brave as she is, she fears the abyss
into which she is slipping. We all fear it.

The next day, very promptly, Dr Sylvester called, another
doctor in the clinic of which Neil is head. Patti also appeared.
Sylvester was bright and sympathetic. He checked Moggins
over, and watched her totter round our low Danish table.
Much three-cornered discussion about which drugs might or
might not help. In the end, he and Patti had to agree that
nothing more could be done. Her leg weakness is the result of
cancerous activity, not coronary malfunction: it is busily gob-
bling up her energies.

She takes all this with great aplomb. She's wonderful. Escorting
Sylvester out to his car, I found he was also admiring.

I received an affectionate if slightly muddled letter from
David Holt. He addressed me as an equal. Wrote back. David is
an intellectual; since his stroke, the emotional aspect of his
nature has found better release.

Father Michael is an entertaining guest. He says he was born
in a northern slum. Somehow, he got to university and became
priest to the Duke of Somewhere (I forget where he said). This
enabled him to shed his youthful suspicion of good manners.
He found that many of the Duke's acquaintances were pleasant
people. We discussed briefly the way in which good manners
can be used very chillingly. Michael is a man of great charm
and character, with a pawky sense of humour. He knows I am a
heathen, but does not seem to hold it against me.

The old situation has changed. I watch with amusement.

Visitors now come to see Margaret. She holds a new fascination for them. I'm the one who serves tea, coffee or wine, according to the time of day. I'm now just Margaret's Husband – an enviable title, I'd say! When I was seeing Dr Sylvester to his car, he regarded me closely, as if he had not noticed me previously. He said something complimentary. I forget what.

By this time, Margaret had had to give up her embroidery, as she had been forced to desert her loom. She left unfinished a fine Uzbek pattern and a rug, as well as an elaborately knitted jacket. I was later to regard these pieces of evidence of her energy and creative power with melancholy. By that time, I was discovering how greatly she was respected and loved by a wide circle of friends with whom she worked. To one of these friends, Rhona Walker, I gave Margaret's unstarted embroidery kit, 'The Strawberry Thief'. Writing to thank me, Rhona said, 'Margaret was always extraordinarily kind to me and I miss her enormously, as I think we all do.'

Such loving messages lit the gloomy days.

Saturday 25th October

It's frosty and bright as yet, with poor air quality. I'm preparing to shop at Sainsbury's, Margaret's in bed, reading the paper. Bless her, she gives me every encouragement, says she's sorry I have to do the shopping.

'No, I love it. I know my way round now.'

'Have fun, darling.'

I'm pretty chipper. Cats are fed. Sotkin is already up on her bed.

But a bad surprise awaited me that evening.

The day had bumped along well enough. I had returned from Sainsbury's and was making another jelly when the bell rang. Alison Soskice, our agreeable neighbour from two doors away, stood at the front door. I let her in, but Moggins was not yet up and about and so could not see her. I gave Alison a sherry and we talked like normal people. This made me happy. I had been reading a booklet Monique had left, *Diets of the Cancer Patient*, which caused me some despair. No help. No solids.

In the afternoon, we went to Blenheim Park, collecting Mark on the way. Margaret is very fond of Mark. We see him all too infrequently. Like me, he is wedded to his job – and his job takes him away from home. We pushed Moggins in her chair by turns. It was cool, but plenty of people were strolling in the grounds, enjoying the sun. Although it was pleasant, it proved difficult to converse with Margaret in her chair. She was apart from us, which I did not like.

Wendy had baked me a pear crumble.

Margaret was exhausted. I wheeled her to the back door. She staggered into the house and lay gasping on the sofa. She had become very frail, and drank a little Marmite.

Well, she hung on there, pretty well prone, watching or snoozing through a documentary on Salvador Dali, the old poseur. She ate an egg and a spoonful of trifle for her supper. After which, I helped her to the stair lift and so up to bed.

There, I sat by her and brushed her hair.

She said, 'I'd like a stay in Sobell House. It's not that you don't take good care of me, I just need the rest. I don't want to have to get up for a while.'

Oh, the harm concealed within those words . . .

She'll never come out of that place. It means the end of our

love, of our marriage, of our life. Despair, despair, wordless
gloom. Of course I agree with her, smile, say I'll arrange
everything.

Later still. Pausing while reading Doris Lessing's *Walking in the
Shade*. Of course I was utterly extinguished by Margaret's
expressing a wish to go into Sobell House. I came downstairs
and howled into the washing up. Yet now – my emotions are
so unstable – only an hour later I find myself not too cast
down. Is it that my adrenalin levels are so high in this crisis
that I feel more alive than usual? Why else do I write these
notes every day, when there is nothing to be told beyond the
simple words: My wife is dying?

The brink, the brink . . . These were to be our last days
together in our little house. Nor did I realise how near to death
she was; perhaps Margaret realised it, and perhaps that knowledge prompted her wish to move into a bed in the hospice.

She now had less than a fortnight to live.

Had I been aware of that, would I have behaved differently? *How* could I have behaved differently? I was her
willing servant.

The move to Sobell House threatened what had become
normality: the two of us together, alone for most of the time,
in our home, still talking to each other, still touching each
other, still breathing the same air.

Sunday the 26th of October marked the official ending of
summer time. Clocks had to be re-set by one hour.

Awakening for her is a slow process, as if part of her already belongs elsewhere. Stages of drowsiness gradually disperse. Her cheeks are quite rosy. Probably the effects of the steroids.

By the time I have set back by one hour most of the house's clocks, and taken up her breakfast on her new tray, she is fully awake and smiling, with a pleasant remark about the sunshine and the solemn church bell. I help her sit up. Her eyes are blue.

She looks doubtfully at the breakfast tray.

'Could I have some tea? Perhaps made with filtered water? Do you still use the filter? Just one teaspoonful of sugar. No Sweetex. Not too strong.'

She thanks me as I go down to boil the kettle. No mention of Sobell.

This little house, which at first I hated, now seems a neat cosy refuge. The rooms are pretty in sunlight. She will never walk in most of them again, but at least they have known her presence.

It's a relief that we're not religious. There's no fervent prayer here, even though congregations locally and in Holt pray for Margaret's soul.

We have no worries about Eternal Life or the Judgement of Sin. You might say Margaret is constitutionally without religion, and untroubled by metaphysical questions. For me it's more hard-fought; I use my scientific knowledge as a barrier against belief in God. I won't let him in. But I'm aware of him always at the door. It must be enough that we're composed of matter forged in the heat of defunct stars. When we die, and are buried or burned, we have a share in a kind of immortality; our component parts go back into circulation, as it were, to recombine in other forms.

> . . . every Hyacinth the garden wears
> Dropt in her Lap from some once lovely Head.

The great and wise Lucretius promulgated this understanding before Christ was born:

> Everything is transformed by nature, and forced into new paths. One thing, withered by time, decays and dwindles. Another emerges from ignominy, and waxes strong. So the nature of the world as a whole is altered by age. The earth passes through successive phases, so that it can no longer bear what it could, and it can now what it could not before.

Despite everything, I persevere with my impossible task of writing an utopia. Half an hour a day. I rejoice that Margaret has read Draft 3.5 and given it her blessing. I fear she will never see it in print. For her, 1998 is an impossible year, the far future, a non-achievable date.

The imaginary dates I describe, towards the end of the twenty-first century, take place long after our deaths. No matter that utopias are impossible in practice; I hope that my vision of one will inspire others with hope and courage.

This has been the day of a thousand years. She decides she cannot possibly get up today.

'I'll have a lazy day,' says my lady, lightly, alleviating for me the harsh truth that she cannot do otherwise.

I bring a plastic bowl and the electric toothbrush for her, so that she can clean her teeth. A small segment of tooth falls off.

With a warm moist flannel I mop her face. She is composed.

Worse is to come. She slides back, closing her eyes. I have to help her to sit up. The bed has become uncomfortable. She begins to cry at her helplessness, she who was always so helpful.

'It has come on so soon,' she says. She implies, rather than stating outright, that she will never see Tim marry in May. It still worries her, and I cannot argue against it.

'Tim will miss your blessing, my love . . .'

'My poor Tim! My poor children! And . . . poor . . .' She cannot get the word out – 'you!'

We are both seized up in a storm of mutual tears.

'Christmas . . . I don't know . . .' More tears.

'I want to live to see my book published.' Again we hug and cry, hug and cry. I tell her that if my passionate love for her had curative power, she would surely live.

'I'll always be with you, darling, always in spirit.'

Later, still weeping, she says that lots of young girls will come round to see me when she is gone.

I deny it. Between us is such an ocean of shared experience, love, adventure, joy, vocabulary: how could anyone else be tolerable?

'Oh, how bitterly I wish I were dying in your place . . .'

We discuss the family. They will look after me, she says. It's all so miserable. We dissolve into tears again. This is our hidden luxury, which no one else sees.

A whole season goes by. Still we weep.

As yet we can still weep together, clutching each other.

Oh, to live that day over again! How happy we were! How we cried!

I recover enough to go downstairs and write to Margaret's so-called publisher. 'Can I convey to you the terrible urgency we feel?' I fax a copy of this letter to Trish. Trish phones back immediately. She will tackle him and get him to pull his finger out.

Alas, as it proves, his digit is inextractable. He does not even have the business sense to get the book out for the Christmas trade.

Lunch of a sort. She must be badly shaken by emotion, as I am. Hours later, I still tremble. Our colloquy went on and on, as we faced the ghastly inevitability of her death. Tomorrow I must phone Patti and Sobell House.

Sleepy time. I lay in a stupor, unsleeping, experiencing uneven heartbeats. She dozed upstairs, awaiting her daughter.

It's wretched always having to greet the children with bad news. I try to tell Chagie it's a mercy that we are given the chance to try to come to terms with this threatened death. And (I find myself yakking on) it is no unusual thing for parents to die before children. At least her mother did not die when she was a child.

Charlotte and I cry together downstairs on the sofa. At length she prepares to go up to talk to Mum. She does not know how to commence the conversation. I suggest, 'I hear you are going to Sobell House?' Then she makes her way upstairs.

I listen to them sobbing together.

Charlotte says she dreams every night of her mother.

When I have driven the sad girlie down into town to meet

Owen, and offered some words of comfort in the car – oh well, the day wears on. By 5.30 it's dark.

I make a jelly with fruit in, which, when set, she more or less enjoys. I lie on the bed with her. We have run out of things to say.

I just feel awful and eat a banana.

Clive rang. He and Youla have arrived in Gatwick. Sorry we can't put them up. Just can't . . .

Turmoil on world's stockmarkets. Think I care?

[VIII]

Charlotte's grief at her mother's condition – hers in particular – was disturbing. Margaret and I had never considered not telling the family, or anyone else, what was wrong. My worry was that she broke her bad news so lightly, and in such a cheerful tone of voice, that the seriousness of the situation might escape our loved ones.

Overlying my deep-seated belief that one does best to face the truth, however unpleasant, was the hope that, by knowing the truth, my children would have a chance to prepare themselves and to speak of their sorrow and love to her who was about to leave us. If they were not told, they would ultimately feel cheated.

There was no ethical dilemma here. Yet the attitude towards death – in particular death by cancer – had become more enlightened of recent years. I found on my shelves a book called *Awareness of Dying*, published in the United

States in 1965. Much of the book discusses how to fudge the truth of oncoming death. Just to give a sample from Part Three, entitled 'The Unaware Family':

> In one case, neither a father nor his son knew that the father would die soon. The attending nurse felt strongly that both should be told, so the father could give the son some last words of encouragement and support and 'bequeath' the many activities that would soon be the son's responsibility. Yet, because doctor's orders forbade disclosure, she was forced against her own feelings to approve the 'meaningless' talk between the two.

There are discussions of 'staff success in keeping the suspicious family unaware'. And, most laughably deadly of all, 'A short blunt announcement may be softened in various ways.' One way is to add a religious flavour: 'You've had a full life now, and God will be calling you soon.'

Such hypocrisy would not have worked on my Margaret!

We never fudged the truth. Nor did any of the doctors we met. Perhaps better medical knowledge and more precise instrumentation have led to a clearer and more truthful approach to the whole alarming subject of death.

On Monday the 27th of October, Roger Carter and his joiner appeared, bearing with them two hand-made doors as specified. One to be fitted between corridor and kitchen – the one Margaret knew about – one between kitchen and dining-room – a secret improvement about which Margaret knew nothing.

I left them to get on with it and did some phoning. I spoke to Clive, who was anxious, as well he might be. I phoned Sobell House and established that a one-bed ward was booked for Moggins for the morrow. There was no time to be gloomy; I prepared Margaret's lunch and chatted with her.

My kind-hearted literary agent, Mike Shaw, arrived, bringing a bottle of Bollinger with him. Unusually privileged, he was permitted to ascend and talk to Margaret while she was in bed. She greeted him with her usual brightness.

In fact, she did well, managing to come down in the afternoon and view – surprise! taa-raa! – *two* new doors.

'Oh, they look very good,' she said in her best admiring style. Clive and Youla arrived, stayed for an hour, and also admired. Those doors were positioned just in time. By the morrow, she would have been gone. The second sofa we had ordered had still not turned up.

Neil phoned during the evening, saying he thought Sobell House was a good idea. What else could he have said – stay away?!

Much more could have been said of today, but I'm too feeble. Irregular heartbeat.

Big fall in stockmarket, Hong Kong and elsewhere.

On the morrow, the day Margaret went into Sobell House, I mentioned in my diary a discussion I had had with Mike. Finding some account of Margaret's illness on her computer eased the rather guilty feeling I had concerning my own day-by-day account. I take it, though, that neither of us could help setting something down, if only to unburden ourselves.

I discussed with Mike the possibility of writing a book about Margaret's illness. Mike was encouraging, and said that the book would be a help to other sufferers.

Any possible book I had contemplated writing I had always discussed with Margaret beforehand. Since it would take about a year to write, it was important we were happy to live with whatever the project was. After much agonising, I tentatively broached to her the subject of dedicating a book to her last months.

Her answer was a knife cutting into my very heart. 'Oh no,' she said, 'I'm not important enough.'

Fancy saying that of oneself! Do you imagine that Mumtaz Mahal made similar protest to the Emperor Shah Johan when he broached his proposal to build the Taj Mahal in her memory? 'Oh no, I'm not important enough'! How I sorrow that Margaret has in her this vein of self-denigration still.

I responded in desperation, wildly, 'There are only two events in my life – the creation of the universe and your illness!'

The cold bites, although lovely winter anti-cyclonic weather still prevails. I've taken a prescription to the chemist's, to get her more enalapril for her heart, that over-taxed heart of hers. She rests. I brew a Douwe Egberts coffee and weep into it, alone.

I've helped her pack a little case.

A penalty for being brave, for never letting a tremor into one's voice when speaking to others, is that they may tell you things you don't wish to hear. Says Neil, 'She may only last two weeks – or she may surprise us . . .'

[IX]

It was on the 28th of October that Margaret was installed in Sobell House at her own request.

Those dedicated people who run Sobell House will perhaps forgive me if I say that the hospice lays no claims to architectural distinction. It is a low, one-storey building with a number of odd angles to it. The resemblance is to a sixties primary school.

Once you are through the revolving glass doors, however, traces of parsimony fade. The place is not silent – nor is it filled with cries of pain. People bustle about, looking cheerful. The wards all lie to the left as one enters. Immediately ahead is a common room, with comfortable chairs and with a facility for visitors to help themselves to tea or coffee – and to wash up their mugs after use.

Part of the vision of Sobell House is to give support to the relations and friends of those who come here to rest and die. I felt that support immediately, and welcomed it. The success of this policy is in part due to the dual nature of the funding. Many of those who work in Sobell are professional; there are also voluntary workers, who act as receptionists, trolley pushers, advisers, cleaners, and I don't know what. The dedication of everyone there is impressive.

Just getting Margaret to Sobell was a struggle. She had to be helped out of bed and into a dressing gown, then down the stair lift. I guided her to the back door and into the wheelchair, where she was covered by rugs. It was all such a tremendous effort for her. As I pushed her to the car, I looked down on her sparse white hair, realising again the bitterness she must feel at having had dwindled into a helpless old woman in two short months.

Then out of the chair into the car. Rugs again. Chair heaved into back of car. Back into house to collect modest case and the tulips Clive had brought her the previous day. Locking up house, wondering if she would ever see it again. On to Sobell House.

There she had a small single ward in which had been installed a brand-new orthopaedic bed, 'The Nightingale'. She could operate the bed, which would recline or sit her up without pushing her down the bed.

Well, it's done . . .

She is now in bed, bright, cheerful, well balanced, perhaps quite enjoying herself. The place is warm, well equipped, and the personnel considerate and kind. I brought her Volvic along but they supply iced water.

I can only write stupidly. I remained by her side for three and a half hours, getting back home after dark, emotionally battered. Clive rang, Tim rang, Wendy rang – she had just been up to Sobell with flowers. Betty rang.

Strangely alone, I ate a double Gloucester sandwich and watched the Channel Four news. The world's stockmarkets appear to have made an amazing recovery. If only *she* could do the same . . .

Will Margaret emerge from Sobell in a week's time? She says she will so confidently that even I begin to believe her – as of course I wish to do.

Perhaps she is even glad to escape from an anguish I can barely conceal.

Charlotte says she dreams of her mother every night. Until last night, I have had no dreams I can remember. Margaret was in bed as usual, knees up. We were in a horrible wooden room, full of bulky unpainted wooden furniture. We decided to enjoy sexual intercourse for one last time. I climbed clumsily on top of her. She could not bear, in the event, to have me up her, or my weight on her. I did not blame her. I stood away. I had no grace, merely felt sad. I woke with an erection. Sat miserably on the side of the bed, holding my head.

Here, now, alone. I come across the last of her many many glasses of water, unfinished. The water goes down the sink. Her smart black summer sandals are in the living-room; they join the neat row of shoes in the back hall. She will never wear them again. Oh, I'm so sad for you, my dearest love, so sad. God bless you always.

Wednesday 29th October

On Margaret's behalf, phoned Rhona Walker, the weaving friend. She sounded enormously fond of Margaret. Of course Margaret's pure clear nature has attracted dear friends; this was one friend I had not met.

Then I phoned Moggins in her Sobell room. That calm lovely voice! She had eaten a Weetabix for breakfast. Unheard of! The tantalising fantasy runs through my head that she will now get better, to emerge from the hospice rejuvenated, and we'll resume our old happy careless life. Oh, if only! If only!

Collecting Clive and Youla from their B&B in Polsted Road, I drove them up to Sobell to see our patient.

Moggins is so snug, so well fed, so kindly attended – how can I compete? She'll not wish to return home at the end of her hypothetical week. Why should she? I'm really sad to think how poorly I've done in the way of care for her. It has become awful and bleak for her at home.

Friendly staff popped in at all times.

Chris was glad to see Clive and Youla; we all stayed about talking for quite a while. After which I drove them back here, to pick up calls on the answerphone and leave messages for Tim and the gardener. The three of us then lunched in the Café Noir – Headington's one slice of Latin Quarter – where Charlotte and Owen joined us. We were quite convivial at a meal for which I paid; not having eaten till then, I enjoyed a salad.

Moggins had a strong desire to see Tim and Charlotte and me together. When I drove Charlotte to Sobell, it was to find Tim already there, DRU parked nearby. Poor Chagie had been very silent on the drive.

M was sitting up brightly in her orthopaedic bed, seeming to enjoy herself. Her courage and good brave spirits never cease to astonish us.

The four of us were all cosy together, as if tomorrow would never come. A pretty young dietician came in and discussed meals; she was humorous too. What did we talk about? To be honest, I have forgotten: ordinary everyday things and incidents of which healthy people talk. We were all happy for a while.

The conversation broke up when genial Dr Twycross arrived to see Margaret. He sat relaxed, as if he had no other thought but her in the world. He stopped the enalapril dosage and halved the steroids. We cleared off and returned home. I took the washing, M's bed linen, in off the line. Chagie fed the cats.

Whatever terrible drama Margaret was undergoing, we were fated to pursue the everyday. Tim, Charlotte and I drove to Wendy's. Clive and Youla came in almost at once. Wendy served a scrummy chocolate cake for tea. We talked about Sobell, and what a brilliant idea it was. The temperature was falling as dusk set in. A simulation coal fire burned bright. The Bainton Road house is very comfortable as a temporary lodging.

Thomas was in good spirits. I drew some nautical adventures for him: swimmers about to be eaten by sharks about to be eaten by bigger sharks, and so on. His small brother is to be christened Laurence Edward Dimitri Lodge.

I rang and wished my wife goodnight. She had had tomato soup and banana custard for supper. *And a G & T beforehand!*

A young pharmacist had visited her in the morning and had taken away the neat little fabric case in which she was accustomed to keeping her drugs. This evening, M reports with some glee, they had mislaid it and its contents.

The pretty dietician unfortunately became interested in Nurishment, which has kept Margaret going since Wendy discovered it in Budgen. I have to take in a sample tin tomorrow for inspection. Nurishment was the ace up my sleeve: one thing that might lure her home! If she can drink it in Sobell, supplied by me, she's all set . . .

Oh well, the poor darling is much better off there than under my care, sad to say.

Rang the sympathetic Rhona, who will go to see M at 3p.m. on Friday. Wendy will go in the morning.

On Thursday the 30th of October, the morning was pleasant and bright, although there had been a heavy frost overnight. I was up and showering before seven, and unlocked the garden gate for the painter, due at eight.

Everything dear was slipping by so rapidly that it already seemed 'normal' that Margaret should be away from home in Sobell House.

At least Tim was at home. His sturdy Toyota off-roader DRU stood in our drive. Tim has become clever at buying, overhauling, reinventing and finally driving these rugged machines, which awaken an echo in his male spirit.

He was sleeping upstairs while I bustled about the house, trying to hold things together. Charlotte was at Owen's place in Cowley. In those days of upheaval, the emotional temperature was warm, even celebratory, because we were together. Chill and silence were to follow soon enough.

Dipping my hand into my old cord jacket pocket, I found, nestling in one corner, Margaret's wristwatch. She'd given it to me for safe-keeping, no longer needing it in the hospice.

I shed many tears over this ornament to her graceful wrist, which for a while retained her individual perfume. Alone in the house, I could not but reflect that when she was gone there would be no one to care for me as she had done – and no one I would be able to love as deeply.

At this time, I had some care of our family in its distress. It remained hard for all to come to terms with the blow that had befallen us. Wendy, Mark and new infant visited Tim and me on this morning. Tim and I had a snack before he headed back to Brighton and work and Sarah.

Scudding about in town, I managed to find Moggins a book she said she longed to read, Lisa St Aubin de Teran's first novel, *Keepers of the House*. When I gave it to her she was pleased.

Whilst in Oxford, plodding the pavement in search of de Teran, I was hailed by a blue-eyed old lady. She greeted me affectionately. It was Roslyn Dale-Harris, in her young days an *Isis* Idol. Later, she published ten romantic novels. Her first husband, John Hale – another *Isis* Idol in his time – had suffered a stroke which had impaired his ability to speak English.

Time is a harsh machine, unremittingly grinding down people's lives.

Clive and Youla arrived home just as I returned. Clive very kindly cut the lawn – a great help. Youla washed up. They were always so thoughtful, and had extended their stay in England until Sunday.

Back in the company of my dear Moggins, I found she had eaten a little lunch. She seemed perfectly content. Her room was banked with flowers. It proved rather difficult to get close to her because of the locker arrangement in her room; there was a slight distancing, as if the role of husband had faded to the inferior one of visitor. She did not seem to mind.

It became a custom with me to get myself a mug of coffee from the common room when I arrived, and to clutch the mug to me. The team that looked after Margaret, among them nurses Rachael Deakin and Stuart Oliver, were always considerate towards the family and me. Stuart has remained reassuringly staunch.

I talked with them while a friendly and amusing Sue gave Margaret a bed-bath, which she enjoyed. She was promised a hair-do on the morrow. The place was busy. Volunteers came round with daily papers, others with tea and coffee trollies, others with alcoholic drinks. Astonishingly, Margaret had another G & T. While at home, she had considered alcohol to be bad for her, apart from the dash of sherry in her soup. Dietary specialists, physiotherapists and doctors visited her, all gentle smiles.

If one cares to be bitter about it, this was the gentrification of death. But why fade out, crumpled on a sack in a barn somewhere? That was not Margaret's style.

Chagie came to see her mother in the afternoon. She followed me to the Volvo in the car park. She is so sad; her sorrow cleaves right through me. I can do nothing. There we stood among the empty cars while she cried on my shoulder. What a terrible misery, cruel to bear. Each of us who loves her suffers in a different way and to a different degree. It bears down particularly hard on Charlotte.

Home to the cats yowling for food, and a smell of paint. The new doors were excellent; but she would never see them in their finished state. A nightie went into the washtub; but at Sobell she had a fresh nightdress every day. Charlotte had bought her a new nightie, very smart.

While I ironed all her bed linen, Clive and Youla went to Sobell House to see her and keep her company. Later, Clive told me of the chill my news of Chris's illness had cast when he had phoned from the seaside resort of Oropos. He was with Youla and her parents and her sister, Poppy. When he broke the news to them, a silence fell upon the hitherto happy party.

During the course of the evening, I rang Margaret to bid her goodnight. She said her supper was not a success. The ground rice had not been ground. A woman in a nearby ward was very noisy. These remarks were delivered as comments on the day, rather than complaints. She sounded drowsily content.

Her closing words were, 'I don't want to leave you, my love.'

This remark I repeated over and over in my head. It showed concern for me, and also resignation, as if she had realised that fight was useless; she might well have said, I didn't want to leave you . . .

No sooner had I put the phone down than it rang. It was Antony in Holt. He and Betty had decided to come to Oxford on Sunday; they would stay in a guest house over the weekend.

There had been a time when, failing properly to understand, I had thought Margaret had no deep feelings, simply because she did not emote in the manner to which Betty and I were accustomed. When I perceived my mistake, I tried to shape my manner to hers; in time – to my benefit – I became cooler and calmer. Now I saw how Margaret's calm demeanour protected her inner self. By this time, I well understood her feelings ran deep about many things, and that she loved me deeply. She was less dependent on the word than I.

So I sat thinking longingly of her in her hospice bed, and of her life, which always seemed so apart from all the violent and terrible things ravaging the world. I strove to feel what she was feeling, knowing she was bound to leave us, we who were so full of life, and this dear bright world of nature. Yet she never let grief overwhelm her.

Oh love, oh my love, you made my happiness, you taught me to be able to be happy and stable. Already I have become less than I was without you near.

Friday 31st October
   This October has been the sunniest since records began, according to the BBC. At least we can be thankful for that.

At the beginning of this month, we were able to drive to
Blakeney with Tim. Her decline has been rapid.

Louise Woodward, an English au pair accused of killing the
baby in her charge, has been found guilty of First Degree
Murder in the American courts. The case has been widely
publicised. She has been given a life sentence, against which
her defence lawyers will appeal.

The painter is here, putting a top coat on the two new
doors. At least they will be shipshape for Bet and Ant.
Otherwise, the house has become strangely still since Tim left.
No GPs, no Patti, no neat little district nurses, no admiring
visitors. The phone rings but rarely.

What would I do without the family painter?!

At home, I learned the meaning of the phrase 'kicking
about'. From this time on, my days were to contain a good deal
of it. After Margaret's death, while tidying up and kicking
about, I found how greatly she had enjoyed making books on
her star subjects. There are notebooks full of her beautiful cal-
ligraphy, or of notes on her various gardens, on furnishing and
decorating houses, and on weaving, as well as on the Jug cui-
sine, already mentioned. As well as the notebooks, there are
Margaret's sketch pads. Perhaps the studies of figures are a little
stilted, but her floral paintings spread uninhibitedly over the
page. All are now treasured and being preserved. I hold them as
evidence of a fulfilled and happily creative life.

My heart is broken. Why do I continue with a record of her
sad, inevitable decline? A wish to remember? At least on this
sunny day she still lives, still responds. When I had to leave her

this morning, we clung wordlessly together, as if I could hold
her back from what must befall.

Nurses attended her, gave her a bed-bath. A physiotherapist
came and coaxed her to sit on the edge of her bed and put her
legs down. M meekly obeyed. There was a big Z-frame to help
her walk, and, steadying herself with this, she managed to
shuffle out into the corridor, turn, and shuffle back to bed,
where she lay resting with eyes closed. How much it pained
her she did not say.

Newspaper sellers come and go, as does the tea man. Sobell
House is quite bustling – surely more lively for her than lying
upstairs here with just me for company. When I enter its doors,
the Sobell atmosphere supports me.

I brushed her hair, which no one else had done. I brought
her some post and a can of Nurishment.

Clive had the bright idea of producing an album of his photos
taken on a holiday we had enjoyed together in Hornbeck, in
Denmark, back in the early seventies. We were delighted to see
them, laughing to see how old-fashioned we looked. Charlotte
then was a sweet ethereal little thing about two feet tall.

Wendy and Thomas had made Grannie some sausage rolls,
with instructions that I should eat them if she couldn't. I had
one for my lunch.

Washed and ironed one of her nighties, and made
preparations for Bet & Ant.

The miserable little crooks who infiltrate a peaceful neigh-
bourhood struck again. Some while previously, I secured an
oval plate showing our house number to one of the stone pillars of our drive entrance. Overnight, some little turd prised it

out and stole it. What for? 'Fun'? To help fund a glue-sniffing habit? Who knows?

But there were more serious things about which to worry.

I could not force myself to work on *White Mars*. I confront a dilemma, rooted in my selfish nature: now that I have endured the misery of her leaving home, am I able to endure it again – as I would if she returns on Tuesday? And if she does return on Tuesday, how can I manage to make her remaining life as happy as is her existence in Sobell? It will be hard – like slavery – to start again on that endless quest for suitable food for her.

Returned to Sobell early evening. Clive and Youla were keeping her company. She had already been visited by Rhona, and seemed tired, slightly slurring her words.

Clive and Youla had brought her a pink knitted bed jacket, which greatly pleased her. I worried about seeming unable to reach her emotionally.

A member of staff delivered a mug of soup. It looked unappetising. Margaret had left her lunch, which had not been entirely cleared away. She took a sip of the soup; that was all. She must be glad of the Nurishment I took her. Tomorrow, I'll take a Marmite sandwich with the crusts cut off, the way she likes it.

She complained rather faintly about the noise in the corridor. I left with Clive and Youla, feeling more upset and worried than usual. We went to eat at Munchy Munchy, an oriental restaurant in town.

Later, Clive gave me serious advice about keeping warm, eating properly, and not attacking burglars. But my appetite has vanished. Food gives me hiccups. I do my share of advice-giving.

When Charlotte rang, I foolishly told her not to be too sad. It
would have been better to have said, 'Admit your deep feelings
of misery.'

Dede and Gary rang from Chicago while I was ironing, to
see how things were. We talked of our happy Exmoor trip just
before the storm broke. Dede said she and Margaret had had a
long intimate talk about mortality. I cut off and weep.

The weary days of October were over. A new month brought
new anxieties. Although I started the days in fairly good
shape, I was generally reduced by the end of them. However,
it did not occur to me, as I rose to greet a forbidding
November, that Margaret had already entered the last week of
her life. Appearances suggested that she had somewhat
revived in the tender care of Sobell House.

Such meditations preceded my morning visit there.

In attempting to fortify myself against what was inevitably
to come, I told myself that one advantage of having no belief
in God was that one could not feel one had been specially
chosen to suffer. If not chosen, then what? That one was
merely a statistic. There was nothing genetically disposing
Margaret to cancer.

The only stance one could take, therefore, was stoicism.
Stoicism and courage seemed to be serving Margaret well,
and would have to serve me.

After all, I had had some training in the knowledge that
the world was bleak. The knowledge had been fortified by
the opening statement of Thomas Hardy's *Dynasts*, that the
Immanent Will worked 'eternal artistries of circumstance,
Whose patterns, wrought in wrapt aesthetic rote, Seem in

themselves its single listless aim, And not their consequence . . .' There was a grain of pleasure to be found in
sustaining oneself in that undeceived view of things.

I drove round to Sobell House, taking with me the
Marmite sandwich wrapped in silver foil. As usual, I parked
where the Volvo could be seen from Margaret's window.

The place was surprisingly quiet. No ladies sat at reception. Unease crept in. Tapping at Margaret's door, I found
Rachael giving Margaret a bed-bath. She did not want me in.
I went and read the *TLS* in the deserted common room until
they were ready.

How worn my poor darling looked, she who I had carelessly
thought would live for ever. She could scarcely manage a
greeting for me. She held my hand and closed her eyes. So we
sat for a while. When at length she roused and opened her
eyes, I saw how yellow the whites had become. Her look was
very distant.

The Marmite sandwich went into her locker for later. She
eats so little. I rescued her can of Nurishment from the
common fridge and poured her some. She did not sip it.

In distress, I turned to the neat little nurse Rachael. She
showed a warmth and concern too little regarded as English.
She also was worried, and took me to speak to the doctor on
duty, a Dr Chambers.

Dr Chambers was young, bright, smart, given to a
psychological approach. He came into the ward and talked to
Margaret. I kept silent, speaking only to prompt her
occasionally. Her mouth was so dry she had trouble speaking
clearly, and sometimes almost sounded drunk. Dr Chambers

listened attentively, observing her uneasy stirrings in the bed, even when she declared she felt very little 'discomfort' – her euphemism for pain.

The doctor immediately increased her diet of co-proxamol, the pain-killer, to five times a day, saying, 'Why should you suffer pain?'

I followed him from the room when he left. We went into a snug interview room and talked together. When I asked about the discoloration in Margaret's eyes, he said that she had 'a slight jaundice'. 'It's a stage the sufferers go through . . .'

Poor lady, as if she did not have trouble enough. [I did not understand; he did not say 'It's the final stage', in order to spare my feelings.]

He admires her fortitude and well understands what I say about her self-abnegation.

'It is difficult to get through to her.' (For some of our early years, I had had the same experience and had retired baffled.) Chambers had read Dr Twycross's notes, and observed that Dr Twycross had 'managed to get through to her'. I knew, however, that her reserve was no façade but integral. How much I would like to read the Twycross notes.

Chambers had studied her body language, which he claimed did not accord with her still light-hearted way of speaking of herself.

We talked for a while. There was some comfort in being able to speak frankly. Because he was acute and sympathetic, I told him of that remark of Margaret's which had pierced my heart: 'I'm not important enough . . .' He shook his head sadly.

Comforting though such conversations may have been, they left one feeling utterly depleted.

Margaret said when I returned to her ward, 'You've been a long while. Have you been talking to the doctor?'

Although I answered with an immediate affirmative, she asked me no further question.

'I'm with you now,' I said, sitting and holding her hand. She closed her weary eyes.

The staff tell me she has expressed every intention of coming home on Tuesday. But she did not walk one step today, and used the commode for her motions.

Returning to Sobell after lunch, I found her asleep, her mouth open, looking extremely unwell, with a bad flesh colour. Not wishing to disturb her rest, I took a walk in the Churchill grounds, of course feeling extremely low.

It's a large area, much of it left to wilderness. I came on a row of ambulances, silent, waiting to rush forth among the populace.

She roused after a while. Smiled, gradually recovered something of her old self. She was glad to see me. Oh my darling treasure, how cruel it is that you should suffer so, and something in the family die with you! I had brought her a present to give Laurence, a snug little coat, the hood of which has animal ears. It pleased her.

She took a drink of water, brightening before Mark, Wendy, Thomas and Laurence arrived.

We were all complacent together, and Wendy suckled her dear baby. Chris held him in her arms.

For my third visit that day, I collected Clive and Youla from the house in Bainton Road. It was foggy and Novemberish everywhere. The world held an air of dull supine anticipation.

Sobell House was very quiet at that time. Margaret was awake and scanning the pages of the *Guardian*. She was glad to see us and quite lively. Some soup had been served, although she hardly seemed interested.

'I may have some later,' she said, in answer to my question. But she was sucking G & T through a straw!

We sat round her bed and enjoyed a pleasant conversation. It was cosy in the room, and adorned with flowers, including a new bunch from Stella, Mark's mother.

Arrangements had to be made for the morrow. Charlotte arrives, and Betty and Antony. Youla and Clive fly back to Greece; it is just as well Clive has a sabbatical year off from teaching at the British Council in Athens, thus being freer to come and go as he will. He and Youla have been terribly kind and concerned, and really have had quite a difficult – well, let's say puzzling – time of it.

As we were leaving, I cradled my dear wife in my arms. She was very affectionate and grateful with me. Although she is not a demonstrative person, I know how deeply she loves me, as I love her.

Clive invites me to share a Chinese takeaway with them, but I could not eat. I said I knew I should be with them.

'There's no "should" about it,' said Clive. 'You go home and rest if you need to.' In his undemonstrative way, he is quite like his step-mother.

The truth is, I need to be alone and silent, and to write

these miserable notes. I will also read Doris Lessing's *Walking in the Shade*, which I think I much enjoy.

8.30. Sitting here uselessly dreaming of her, I decided to ring and wish her goodnight. She sounded so remote, her clear little voice so tiny, so tired. Oh my darling, it's happened so fast.

But we could never have time to adjust to such a disaster, could we?

Silly hiccups. Sensation of indigestion, although I've eaten next to nothing. Can't swallow the idea of Moggins's illness?

There is a possibility I could sleep in Sobell, to be close in case of emergencies.

Sunday 2nd November.

This was the day Clive and Youla were to fly back to Athens. And the day that Betty and Antony arrived. I had booked a small hotel room for them.

At present, Margaret's drugs are as follows, as far as I can discover:

dexamethasone . . . steroids

domperidone . . . anti-sickness

diazepam . . . for sleep

Luborant . . . mouth moistener

and increased doses of co-proxamol.

On this morning, I arrived at Sobell House shortly after nine, to find my lady sitting smiling by her washbasin, while Rachael washed her hair. Going to get myself a coffee, I found a family weeping in the common room. Not unusual, one must understand.

When I went back into her ward, it was to find her lying

snug in her Nightingale bed, with banked pillows bulging like bags of flour behind her head. Her delicate feet were out to cool at the foot of the bed. She wore a spotless nightdress and her new pink bed jacket.

Her eyes were closed. Her colour was not as good as it had been.

She was the picture of an invalid. I kissed one of those feet which had become tender with rest.

She stirred and murmured a greeting. The languor that now surrounded her was untypical, unlike the courtesy with which she still greeted her visitors. We must all tax her.

The fresh-faced, clear-eyed Rachael was admirable and capable. Since Margaret wished to doze, I went with her and Stuart to a study room. There we discussed how much longer Margaret had, and whether she really wished to return home. We believed that she did.

There were difficulties about her return on Tuesday. In Margaret's state, I would no longer be able to manage single-handed; assistance and assistants had to be organised, which would take time. Bed-elevators were needed, zimmer-frames, commodes . . . And of course nurses . . . Nurses day and night. It had got to that stage.

Both Rachael and Stuart were calm, grave, helpful. I thought how pleasant it would be to lie with Rachael in my arms. Such naughty thoughts could not be helped, and I brushed them away.

After this discussion, Rachael and I returned to Margaret's ward, to find her awake. Rachael explained to her about the problems of organising proper assistance. Margaret listened, seeming to be unperturbed. Finally, Rachael suggested she stayed for a few more days. Margaret acquiesced (as, I reflected later, she had so often acquiesced for the convenience of others). She would not mind staying for a few more days.

I asked her if she would not prefer to stay in Sobell. When she responded that she wanted to come home, I inwardly rejoiced. She closed her eyes again.

Charlotte and Owen arrived. So I left.

This was a foggy day. I worried to imagine Antony, never a particularly confident driver, driving Betty over from Norfolk. It was bold of them to come. I looked forward to seeing them again; but it was another item to occupy my attention. They would stay till Tuesday.

In the afternoon, I was to have the whole family to tea at Hambleden. I went into town and bought biscuits and a glutinous strawberry cake. Following the tea, Clive and Youla would have to catch a coach to the airport.

Betty and Antony arrived in good fettle. The fog had cleared by the time they reached Peterborough. They had eaten lunch on the way – or at least Betty had. I gave them each a Glenfiddich.

When we reached Sobell House, we found Margaret asleep. We sat and talked over coffee in the common room until Rachael roused Margaret at three. We went in and all was smiles. She seemed quite bright. I introduced Bet and Ant to some of the staff. While we were chatting, Antony spoke of a letter to *The Times*; two elderly dons were walking together in Oxford's High, and one was overheard saying to the other, 'And ninthly . . .'

As we left, Chagie and Owen were arriving. And when we

reached number 39, we found Clive and Youla waiting there. Wendy, Mark, Thomas and Laurence soon poured in. Good old family! Everyone had brought a cake for the tea party. We were all cheerful or feigning to be so.

The babe looked fine. Clive, Chagie and others had a nurse of him, in pass-the-parcel mode.

Thomas enjoyed the stair lift, as did Wendy. Thomas had already learnt to work the mechanism himself, laughing at his own success.

The tea itself was also a success, with Charlotte presiding over the teapot, and all animated. But Clive and Youla had to leave. We piled into the car with all their luggage, and I drove them to the station. Tim was going to meet them at Gatwick.

They gave me many instructions to look after myself. Although we were sad to part, I suspected they would be back again soon.

At 8.30, I rang my dear Moggins to wish her goodnight. How small and forlorn sounded that dear voice.

That night, after a crowded day, terror seized me. The jaundice marked a further deterioration of her liver. Not an illness in itself, it marked an increase in her real disease. Supposing she was dying in the night – would Sobell ring me, so that at least I could be with her and hold her hand?

Talking to Stuart today, I asked him to make a note that I be called.

'Of course, we don't know when it will be,' he said. 'It may not be in the next few days.'

Oh, great! That was fine, then! We needed not worry in that case . . .

Why did I fool around, obeying a social impulse, instead

of just remaining with her by her bedside? It might have been that I could not bear to do so. The rest of the family were all adults, well able to look after themselves.

One did not know what to do, or what might be done . . . The encroachment of death, the negation of reason throw reason into confusion. My diary says:

> . . . she is dying inch by inch. She can hardly speak for that dry mouth, but she still remembers she loves me. It's an old habit. Moggins, my darling girl, no one ever loved me as you do, and I don't deserve a half of it. Although I fear the responsibility, I want you back here, to care for you in your last few precious weeks!

Weeks? I still hadn't got it, had I?

And so we all managed to reach the 3rd of November. Betty and Antony were being extremely considerate. It was a pleasure to have their company, even in the strained circumstances. Antony went out into the garden once an hour to smoke a cigarette, the habit he cannot break. That morning, his inspiration was to pick a posy for Margaret from the flowers and plants in our garden: a tuzzy-muzzy, as he calls it. 'Tuzzy-muzzy' was an expression Mary Shelley used.

We entered Margaret's ward. She looked very elegant, propped up by clean pillows and in a clean nightdress. As ever, she was smiling and courteous, and seemingly cheerful. How much I wished to have her to myself, to talk confidentially. However, this was a semi-social occasion; I could not invite her inner thoughts. She was fatigued, and often spoke with closed eyes.

It was a pity there was no one from the Manson side of the family to visit her. The Aldiss side certainly made up for the lack.

Antony claims a special bond with her, since he and she were both adopted Aldisses. 'She's a loving person – and asks nothing for it,' was his verdict. I did not dispute it; but I knew well that for the harmony we had enjoyed for many years it was necessary that both sides had to demand and give something.

Then there were various matters to be attended to: Bet and Ant to be driven into town, Margaret's correspondents, some very anxious, to be answered, and some preparations to be made for a TV interview I had agreed to do in easier times. Adding to the distractions, an occupational therapist came to Hambleden with an assistant to install a bed erector in Margaret's bed. It was quite an old-fashioned, cumbersome thing. I asked for an oxygen cylinder as well; that, I was told, was more of a problem.

I managed to wash and iron some of my shirts and her nightdresses. Liz, the chiropodist, came to tend my feet, and was sympathetic.

Then the TV invasion for a couple of hours. A young woman, Polly, interviewed me regarding science fiction and prophecy, as if she at least regarded the subject as important. Now that the USA, more than ever, has become the meta-centre for SF, novels and movies of science fiction are present-day mythologies of power.

Betty and Antony returned while the filming was going on. Once the team had left, Antony volunteered to cook supper, although he eats so little himself. At this stage, I was indifferent to food. I was so crazed with worry about Margaret that the rest of life was a blur; it was as if I was caught in a fast current and could only watch helplessly as the coastline rolled by. There lay my gorgeous wife, alone; I had to get back to see her.

It was dark. I parked the Volvo opposite her window and went in.

She was dozing, and vague when she awoke, though as ever pleasant and affectionate, without complaint. I held her to me without words. So we stayed.

I asked her what she was dreaming about.

'Oh . . . muddled . . .' That was her gentle murmur.

On her side-table, her slender lunch of soup-in-a-mug and ice-cream stood untouched. The Marmite sandwich wrapped in its silver foil lay untouched in her locker. When I asked her, she said she had not been out of bed all day.

I went to complain. Could not someone have sat by her for five minutes and have coaxed her into taking a little nourishment? Why had the physiotherapist not helped her to take a dozen steps with the Z-frame?

Dr Chambers and I sat in the same study we had used before. He was patient in explanation, and bleak his explanations were. Margaret, he said, had reached the stage where she no longer wished for nourishment. Also, she was perhaps too weak to wish to walk. My heart thudded irregularly within its cage, as if it would burst free.

These *stages* . . . These steps down into her personal darkness . . .

The doctor, speaking to her earlier in the day, had asked

her how it felt to be doing so much dozing. Her reply had startled him.

'Lovely,' she had said.

He repeated the word for my benefit. *Lovely*.

He had asked her if she wished to leave Sobell House and go home, or to remain where she was.

Her reply was cautious and strange.

'We'll have to wait,' she had said.

Chambers said it was possible that the regular doses of diazepam were having a cumulative effect. He would halve them and see if it made a difference.

When I asked about the chances of my sleeping in Sobell, he said it was possible; it could be arranged.

Alas, alas, it seemed the end was near. Should I take her to die at home, or leave her in comfort where she was? I could not then arrive at a decision.

I went back to hold her hand and kiss her feet and talk to her. It was not a very coherent conversation. She was only half-awake. Tears rolled quietly from my eyes. This darling woman and I had shared half our lifetimes together, and in my case at least it had been beyond doubt the happier, freer part. So many seasons we had seen together and rejoiced in.

I held her and kissed her and murmured endearments, to which she responded with gratitude.

Seeking out a kind nurse, I got her to track down a pot of Marmite in a pantry cupboard. Margaret would drink Marmite if she could drink anything. Well, it was something. Something to do.

My habit was, when I left the building, to go to her window and tap farewell with my car key. She would respond by flashing her light on and off. This she managed to do on that occasion.

I drove back to Betty and Antony. Antony had cooked salmon en croûte. They were both kind and supportive. I walked with them back to their B&B. Then I was alone and the day was done.

Now it's 10 p.m. and the old torture: is she going to live through the night? Oh Lord, in whom I cannot believe, please save my dear love! Spare her for a few weeks more.

Two shards from the broken day. Margaret asked Antony how his client June was. June also suffers from cancer. She has now quarrelled with Antony – and remains alive.

Betty's sharp eyes noted that Margaret had read nothing more of Keepers of the House. The effort of reading has become too much.

There's no way I can express my sorrow – not to Margaret, not to the family. Not even to myself.

In those first evenings alone, there was time enough to look back over Margaret's and my long association. It could be said, and indeed many said it, that fate was cruel. But fate is a random factor, and that factor had favoured me in the past, not least in arranging that Margaret and I met, and fell in love. At that time, my fortunes were low. They improved with remarkable speed once we were together.

I took pleasure in recalling some of our special times. One of Moggins's cleverest tricks was to secretly organise a sixty-fifth birthday party for me at the Groucho Club in London. How she managed to keep this elaborate festivity a secret, working in collaboration with Frank Hatherley and Malcolm Edwards, I will never know.

We went to London by train. I entered the Groucho all innocence, only to find myself in the midst of a great celebratory party. Members of the family, like sheepdogs rounding up the flock, had shepherded such distinguished friends as Kingsley Amis, Harry Harrison, Mike Moorcock, Doris Lessing and others in from a nearby pub. Even more wonderful, Clive had been flown in from Greece for the occasion. In they all paraded and speeches were made.

Even more astonishing, Margaret had organised and published a book, amusingly called *A is for Brian*, full of messages and absurdly warm praise from many good old friends.

Fun and junketing went on, until a company of us retired upstairs for dinner. But the element of that enjoyable occasion I enjoyed most – and which surprised me most – was to see and hear Margaret speaking in public, humorously and with absolute confidence. She had had great delight in arranging the whole evening. A marvellous conjuring trick.

Three years later, on the occasion of her sixtieth birthday, I was able to spring a surprise on her. I wrote a play for the family to act, a comic version of Shakespeare's *The Tempest*, full of family references. The family was left to rehearse and arrange everything while Moggins and I went off to Greece for a holiday. I had secretly already bought our costumes and my disgusting long wig.

We had invited Betty and Antony over for the occasion but they could not come. Margaret formed the entire audience for *The Mock-Tempest*, performed in the garden on her birthday, 23rd May, under the old oak tree. Charlotte was Miranda, Mark was Prospero, Wendy (then pregnant, did we but know it) was Ariel, Tim was Prince Ferdinand, Charlotte's boyfriend Gerry was the sea captain, and Tim's girlfriend Helen was Ceres. I grabbed the chance to play the role for which nature had designed me, Caliban.

In conclusion, Ceres darted on and spread a rug on which plates and cake were laid. Cast and audience sat down and had tea there and then. Oh yes, we regarded each other as special.

But now . . . no more cakes and ale? Well, perhaps never again such gladsome days. However, two months after Margaret's death, when I had felt like death myself, I woke to find curiosity stirring.

Blessed curiosity. Margaret would not have wished me forever mourning, forever wretched. Perhaps I had absorbed by example some of her courage. In any case, I found within myself a nestling curiosity – perhaps a novelist's curiosity – as to what would happen to me next . . .

It must mean that life was reviving within me, however reluctant I was to acknowledge the fact. And I accepted an invitation to dinner with friends.

Tuesday 4th November

    4 a.m. Cannot sleep. I wander the house, full of desperation. At least if she were here I could hold her to the last. Why did I once fear having her back?

    What is she feeling at this moment? Does she feel deserted? I see she is releasing her hold on the world. The time will come when she must also release me. I dread being let go.

Should I rush to her side now, just to see her again, to be in that little room with her?

We built such communion together. I think again of her on the sofa with me, her pure look of complete trust in me. All the miseries and insecurity of my early life were forgotten. Now they return to lend weight to present grief.

Evening. A hard day, I'd judge. Hard for everyone. Much anxiety in the family. Tim drove up from Brighton, but had to return in the afternoon to work. Chagie rang; she will be here to see Mum tomorrow.

It should be noted here that both Tim, working in Brighton, and Charlotte, working in Bath, put in long hours at their respective jobs. Margaret and I felt they had hard task-masters. So it might be. Yet both were given compassionate leave for some days away from work when it was understood that their mother had died.

This is an indication of a civilised society.

I waved Bet and Ant off with regret – some regret, anyhow, since it is easier not to eat and easier to skulk here alone of an evening. Ant is much upset, so much so that he has become again unable to take food. Betty says he has written a letter to Margaret.

A change in Sobell House, and not one for the better. This morning, I found Margaret sitting out of bed, looking bright, while Rachael washed her and made her bed. This evening, I found her in a different bed, a rather inferior one. The Nightingale had flown. She lay on her side, huddled up, her head low. She slept.

It's clear even to me that she is in a poor way. The deterioration during her week in the hospice is marked. Is it the cancer or the co-proxamol that makes her so dozy? One does not know what to expect. She took no nourishment – not even Nurishment. She did not eat the little sandwich I made. She had only sips of water. When I complained about this I was told again that 'people go through this stage'. However, sitting by her bedside and trying to converse with her, I learned that she might enjoy some milk. When I brought some from the common room, she was able to drink and clearly felt glad of it.

She could speak so little, and scarcely opened her eyes. I just held her hand. Yet she seemed content – happy, one might almost say, as if her spirit were remote from the trying circumstances. It was a relief to be alone with her. Her legs were restless, although she declared herself perfectly comfortable.

Perhaps in some of her dreaming slumbers she imagined herself back again in Tibet, in God's great world of mountains and monasteries. To that remote country she had travelled in 1987, accompanied by Edith Holt, Beverley Strickland and other friends, mainly American. The ladies lived hard, crossing dangerous landslips on foot, and enduring primitive conditions. They had visited the Potala Palace in Lhasa. In all, the party was away from England for a month; Charlotte and I lived on our own in Woodlands; it was strawberries-and-raspberries-and-cream time, and we did it justice.

That trip, away from me, away from the family, away from domesticity, had a profound effect on Margaret. Our Volvo sported a 'Free Tibet' sticker for many a year afterwards; Margaret gave money to the Tibetan cause and subscribed to their journals. At one period, we attended a course on Buddhism, and obeyed its silences and meditations. We collected books on Tibet, old and new. Tibet, with its pure air, was an important station on Margaret's spiritual journey through life.

She would be happy to return there, if only in the world of dream . . .

Preparations continue to bring her home on Thursday or, more likely, Friday, when everything will be ready for her. I have overcome my qualms and am positive about having her home once more, if she still wishes to come. An ambulance will be made available.

During a long discussion with the admirable Dr Twycross, he said patients often desire to return home with the objective, possibly only subconscious, of saying their farewells to it.

Useless to write, unless to scribble these notes. My life has stopped. I don't know myself. Ponderous heartbeats.

It was at this time Margaret received a card of good wishes from Deborah and Nicholas, the couple who lived in our old home, Orchard House. Was Margaret a sentimental person? Certainly, she felt a strong link of affection for Deborah, so lately met, so briefly known. Perhaps she saw in her, with the babe at her breast, something of herself when young, happy in that pleasant place.

We lost Orchard House through the negligence of our then accountants. Suddenly we found ourselves owing an immense amount of back tax. Our accountant arrived in his white Rolls Royce to try to restore the damage; but nothing could be done to meet the debt except sell the house and the science fiction collection I had amassed.

Margaret was upset by this turn of events.

'Don't worry,' I said. 'It's not as bad as if we had broken our legs. I'll write another novel.' It was my turn to be cool.

Through the good agencies of the booksellers, Bertram Rota Ltd, the science fiction collection was sold to Dallas Public Library. I flew to Dallas to attend the official opening of the Aldiss Collection. Dallas was lovely, with adventurous modern architecture, and the local SF fans were an hospitable bunch.

Margaret had said blithely before I left home, 'Please don't go buying me anything, but remember if you do that I'm into chunky gold jewellery.' I was full of the feel-good factor, and entered the doors of the famous Nieman Marcus store, where in the foyer (or do I exaggerate?) were two gold-plated helicopters labelled His and Hers. There I bought a splendid chunky gold bracelet designed in Paris.

Margaret was delighted with it, often wore it, and willed it to Wendy when she died.

Long after the funeral, going to her desk, I found there a white rectangular box, empty, with Nieman Marcus inscribed on it. There it lay, after three house moves. Yes, Margaret was sentimental. Her dear heart was easily touched.

All the family have either phoned or been phoned. Wendy has additional problems. Thomas's nursery school has closed unannounced. Now she has difficulty finding another. All the Oxford schools are already full.

Wendy said that she had spent a very happy half-hour with Chris yesterday. Chris had nursed baby Laurence. She told

Wendy that she was quite content, and that when she was
home again she would be able to walk from her bed to the
stair lift, and perhaps get out in the garden again.

Quite content . . . She is a truthful lady. We must believe
what she said. Her hopes, however, did not bear the stamp of
realism.

My sweet girl is *in extremis* now. No doubt of that. But at
least she still lives. When she has gone . . . oh well, my
emotional life will be sucked into the black hole with her. How
could it possibly be otherwise?

In my eyes, she was always so beautiful, so elegant. Her skin
was so fine. During our early years, I sought to get emotionally
nearer to her, desisting when she said, *Don't try to come too
close.* Although I might have regretted that aloof quality, it
found an echo in something in my own character.

Now she is even further from me, entering her own world.
Her wretched experience with her so-called publisher is
forgotten. Perhaps she does find herself in a world of dreams
that is *lovely.* We must hope so.

I dreamed that I was in a strange town, searching, searching
for her. Once I caught sight of her in a dark blue dress, but she
disappeared.

[X]

We have little choice regarding when or how we die.
Thinking about it afterwards, I grieve that my beloved wife
died at such a comparatively young age, when she was so

content, so vital; and yet there was some mercy in her going, if she had to go. Our shock and outrage at her illness would have been much greater had death come without warning – shall we say, by a stroke, or in a road accident.

Or supposing England was a less peaceful, more sectarian country, and Margaret had been shot by some unknown man in a balaclava for being a Catholic, or, as she actually was, an Unbeliever – that violence would have been far more lacerating. Our sense of the inate cruelty of life would have bitten deeper.

On the other hand, had she suffered from an illness that incapacitated her for years, perhaps with a loss of her mental powers, from ME or from CJD, then the strain on the family would have been even greater; we would have been – although this is hard to imagine – even more miserable than we were.

There are no good deaths. But cancer of the pancreas, it must be admitted hindsight, is not the worst of them.

The day before she died, Wednesday the 5th of November, was showery with heavy downpours at times. The long drought was ending.

It proved to be a day of crisis – of change and anxiety.

When I arrived at Sobell, it was to find Margaret lying on her side, sound asleep. She hardly roused all day. I sat there for a while, could not stay, went to get coffee from the common room, walked about, returned. Still she lay there.

She and I never achieved any intelligible exchange that day, although Mark and Charlotte, when they came, were more fortunate.

'My poor girl!' Margaret said distinctly, twice.

Mark says that a tear spilled from her closed eye.

Seeing my anxiety, Rachael invited me to a small conference room, where she allowed me to talk. My emotions ran
so high, I found myself saying that life was a quest for love,
stability and knowledge, and that I had enjoyed the good fortune to find these things in my second marriage. That I had
hardly recognised my fortune at first, that later I always strove
to deserve it, that Margaret fulfilled all my dreams of what a
marriage could be . . . That she was a splendid wife and
mother. That she was always so attractive. That it seemed a
wicked misfortune that she should be struck down in the
happy years of her maturity, when otherwise we had had few
cares and a contented family, to which she was central . . .
And so on. I could not check myself from uttering the words.
Yet I spoke measuredly, with scarcely a tear in my eye.
Rachael listened to the burning account patiently.

That morning, it was still assumed that Margaret would
return home on Friday. Elaborate arrangements were being
made for various nurses and back-up teams to come. Charlotte
and I brought back a zimmer frame and commode in the car
at lunchtime. We ate sandwiches here, without appetite.

The gardener arrived. I left Charlotte to cope with, and
pay, the cleaners, while I returned to Sobell. Monique arrived
late, caught up in work.

By 5.30, Patti Pugh arrived and took stock of the dismay-
ing scene. I was now informed that Margaret had endured a
crisis in the night. Constipation had stopped her excreting.
Apparently, bowels still fill with faeces even if you have ceased
to eat. She was in pain. They gave her a suppository and
shots of morphine. She was now on morphine, or a deriva-
tive, rather than co-proxamol.

So she had remained almost comatose all day.

After considering these circumstances, Patti decided that Margaret should return home on the morrow, Thursday, rather than on Friday, as had been planned. She implied that Friday might be too late. This proved a wise decision.

A meeting was held. Rachael, Sue, Monique and Patti were present, wishing to hear my judgement. I had no qualms in saying that I wanted Margaret home, because I believed that that was what she wanted. She could die in my arms.

However ill she might be, she would wish to say goodbye to the home on which we had worked so hard, and to the cats, the garden, the whole ambience. The cycle would be completed.

I was positive with the ladies. They promised to supply back-up. They were marvellous.

Margaret did not rouse. Low in spirits, I left her there. That evening, I did not tap with the car key on her window. I went and sat in the car and cried helplessly. I got myself back home through a rainy Guy Fawkes night. Chagie, Wendy and Mark were all there.

I rang the Rev. Michael Brewin.

John Stanton rang.

John and Trish Simms rang.

I rang Harry.

Betty rang.

All were glad to know Margaret was coming home. Meanwhile, she slept on, thanks to diamorphine 20.

Thursday 6th November

    Woke just after seven, showered, feeling amazingly

cheerful. Whatever difficulties are involved, never mind, my
dear wife comes home to me today.

Evening. Perhaps it's lack of prescience which permits
cheerfulness. Directly I reached Sobell House, I saw how deeply
ill Margaret was. The jaundice had progressed. She could not
open her eyes. She breathed heavily through an open mouth,
and her colour was bad.

She was in a state which would probably be described as
comatose, although when I spoke to her, held her hand,
stroked her cheek, she was aware of my presence.

She was connected to a diamorphine trigger to keep the
pains of disintegration at bay. A catheter had been fitted; a
brownish liquid drained into a plastic container by her
bedside.

The male nurse, Stuart, was clearly concerned by her
condition. He wanted to know if I thought it wise to move her.
Charlotte arrived providentially. She remained calm and was a
fine support for me. The two of us went into a consultation
room with both Stuart and Patti. We were all in a state of high
anxiety. My heart was in an uproar.

It was Patti, the Macmillan nurse, who had brought forward
Margaret's homecoming from Friday; I will always be grateful
to her for that foresight. Now she appeared nervous and – for
once – indecisive. She told Charlotte and me clearly that there
was a chance that if Margaret was moved she might die in the
ambulance.

We found ourselves forced to talk the situation over and
over, it seemed in slow motion. More than once, Charlotte and
I had to say that we wished to take Margaret home because

that was the wish she had repeatedly expressed. She had expressed it clearly to Wendy as recently as the previous Monday afternoon.

So Patti and Stuart were persuaded. I clapped Stuart on the shoulder as we left the room, and hugged Patti, as she had once hugged Margaret, wordlessly.

The decision was cleared. Charlotte and I stood around in a great state until the ambulance arrived. The crew, a man and a woman, lifted Margaret from her bed on to a stretcher and carried her out to the vehicle. Charlotte and I travelled home with her.

We gave her a running commentary on where we were going and what we were passing. Charlotte held her hand. She still lay there, mouth open, eyes closed, breathing with difficulty. Yet we were certain that a part of her was aware.

I am writing against time, and cannot detail all the trouble and pain of that morning. Members of the family came round. Mark and Wendy remind me that I was concerned for Thomas; the shock of seeing someone die should not be inflicted on a three-year-old; although death is a part of life, the transition from one state to the next is hard for anyone to bear, not least a child of fine sensibilities. The ambulance drew into our side drive. Then there was the problem of getting Margaret upstairs and into bed. Another ambulance arrived, with two paramedics. Patti was there, and a rather wild-looking but immensely kind district nurse. I suppose everyone was distraught to a degree. Eventually, they took Margaret from her stretcher and put her in a chair, which was then lifted from the ambulance and carried upstairs. Finally, she was established in her own bed.

There she lay, breathing heavily, eyes closed, mouth open, scarcely recognisable.

Tim and Sarah arrived. Wendy and Mark arrived, with Laurence. All were here who could get here. Clive and Youla were flying back from Greece.

Macramé climbed on to the bed and sat meekly at Margaret's feet, purring.

It became obvious to us all that my darling – our darling, I should perhaps say – was having to make her long farewells to life as well as home. We talked to her, reassured her that all were here and loved her. Neil arrived. Nothing could be done. It was good of him to be there.

So we sat, watching her, keeping vigil. The diamorphine feed was continuous, the catheter bag by the bedside continued to fill with a dark bloody liquid. When her breath began slightly to rattle, I became frightened and phoned Jackie, the district nurse, who had left only half an hour earlier. We all sat about, anxious, partly dumb in the face of advancing death. We held her hands. She was growing cold. We told her where she was. She understood she was home.

Sadly, no one can tell what might then have been in Margaret's mind. I believe there was only tranquillity. She would share our feelings of comfort that she was lying at home. Perhaps she imagined she was a girl again, walking with her cousin in the Ochils in Scotland.

Perhaps she was reliving – who knows? – the early days of our love, when she had been so beautiful and her mixture of shyness and determination so marked. Perhaps she even remembered the Titty Dance.

I ran down into the garden and cut a sprig of the sweet flowering choisia growing by our back gate. By squeezing a leaf under her nose, I hoped she could smell that pungent aroma; it would confirm where she was. The rest of the sprig I set in a vase by her bedside.

The end came on as steadily as the advance of evening. I cradled my dying love in my arms, talking to her, kissing her pallid brow.

Her colour became corpse-like, filled with unnamed shades.

Suddenly, her eyes opened. They were blurred, and unlike her eyes. She stared ahead, some said afterwards she looked at Wendy. Then they finally closed.

Her breathing became quiet, each breath slower than the last, with terrifying pauses between.

'One more breath, my darling!' I begged. She delivered it. Her breaths became few and slight. Far between. I held her gently.

She ceased to breathe. It was about 3.55.

We all wept and tried to comfort each other. Neil was there at the last. Chagie was choked with sorrow. Tim said it was the first time he had seen anyone dead.

We all went downstairs.

Patti and Jackie settled Margaret more comfortably in the bed and tied up her jaw with a chiffon scarf. When I took myself upstairs again, Wendy was sitting by the bedside in sorrowing vigil. The nursing ladies had found the sprig of choisia, and arranged Margaret clutching it.

Her body will stay here with me overnight. I will sleep

beside it. The undertakers will come in the morning to take her mortal remains away.

And then we shall all live in a world of 'Never again'.

Margaret's funeral took place on the 12th of November, in the parish church of St Andrew's, in St Andrew's Road, Headington – only a few hundred yards away – presided over by our kindly local vicar, Father Michael Brewin. The grand old church was filled with mourners, people who had known and loved her.

Margaret had chosen the hymns and the music. Alex Duncan read Thomas Hardy's sonnet, 'She to Him' . . . 'When you shall see me in the toils of time, My lauded beauties carried off from me . . .'

The organ played Bach's chorale, '*Ich ruf zu dir, Herr Jesu Christ*', a lovely piece we had encountered years earlier, in Denmark, at a showing of Andrei Tarkovsky's film *Solaris*.

Charlotte had bravely elected to say a few words, so Wendy and I did the same.

Margaret's body was buried in Headington Cemetery after the ceremony. It was Wendy who thought to bring a posy to the grave. She handed me a share. We threw the flowers down on Margaret's coffin before the soil closed over it.

[XI]

These are the tributes we paid during the church service.

Brian:

Despite her beautiful clear English voice, Margaret was a Scottish lass. She had the misfortune to be born in Maidstone, Kent. Both her parents were unmistakably Scots; her father worked under Beaverbrook in the Air Ministry during the war. Margaret began to train as a ballet dancer, which perhaps goes some way to explain her graceful movements, but she was deemed too tall.

Some of you knew Margaret perhaps only slightly. You can't fail, though, to have received the impression of a brave, clear-sighted, kindly personality. She possessed that blessing, a tranquil and happy spirit, which even marriage to me could not disrupt. How well she withstood our frolicsome parties and my terrible friends!

It's notorious how awful is marriage to an author. Yet Margaret managed to produce three books of her own, don't forget. A celebratory book called *A is for Brian* (the poor dear could never spell), a 360-plus page bibliography of my work, and her delightful Boars Hill anthology, still unpublished. All done – everything done, even her dying – without fuss or unnecessary display.

Margaret was my second wife. We lived in harmony. I had two children by my first marriage, Clive and Wendy, whom I greatly love. Margaret, without attempting to usurp a mother's role, took them under her wing and loved them. I suppose she must have thought initially that if she could put up with me, she could put up with them. But she did love them 'like her own', as the saying is, and they loved her. And when our own joint children were born, all four children became one family – I say it with awe and astonishment, and gratitude to them all – without jealousy or quarrels. So it's remained. Charlotte was born punctually on the spring morning of Wendy's tenth birthday. It was just one of Margaret's miracles . . .

Many are the happy times we've all enjoyed together, in France, Scandinavia, Jugoslavia, er – Belgium, and elsewhere.

Our family is a wonderful testimony to affection, forbearance and love. She who engendered these bonds has now left us, taken by cancer in her sixty-fourth year. A Czech friend only last year referred to Margaret as 'eternally youthful'. So we shall always remember her.

I want to read you a short piece from Walter Savage Landor's *Imaginary Conversations*, which has haunted me since I came across it over half a century ago. It's a pagan lamentation about the frailty of the human condition.

Laodameia died; Helen died; Leda, the beloved of Jupiter, went before. It is better to lie in the earth betimes, than to sit up late; better, than to cling pertinaciously to what we feel crumbling under us, and to protract an inevitable fall.

We may enjoy the present, while we are insensible of infirmity and decay; but the present, like a note in music, is nothing but as it appertains to what is past and what is to come.

There are no fields of amaranth on this side of the grave; there are no voices, O Rhodope, that are not soon mute, however tuneful; there is no name, with whatsoever emphasis of passionate love repeated, of which the echo is not faint at last.

Charlotte:

On a couple of occasions, during what turned out to be your last weeks with us, and in fact during the last conversation we had, Mum, you said to me, 'My poor girl, my poor girl!' So now here we are, poor, and indeed wretched without you.

But my brother Tim and I, and Wendy and Clive, had the richest and luckiest life possible, with you to care for us and love us.

Now we are left with many happy memories of the loving home and family you created for us; of happy times in Oxford, carefree summers in Norfolk and travelling around Europe – indeed places, many of which reminded you of Scotland.

Tim and I have planted a tree in your memory. How you would have laughed to see us trying! I'm afraid neither of us seems to have inherited your natural gardening talent. But what will live on, if only in our memories, will be your selflessness, your sense of family, and your good sweet nature.

We are lost without you, Mum. May golden slumbers kiss your eyes.

Wendy:

I am sure that anyone who was lucky enough to know Margaret will have a special memory of her. As her step-son and -daughter, my brother Clive and I have always called her by her other Christian name – Chris – so that is the name I shall use today.

Chris had many qualities and virtues. Today I would like to remember two ways in particular in which she enriched my life.

The first affected me most in my childhood, and this was Chris's genius at making everything 'all right' again. Incidents and situations which to a young child seemed catastrophic she handled with care and kindness and miraculously turned into events that could be looked back on fondly. Using her example, I will try to do the same for her grandchildren, Thomas and Laurence.

As an adult, I came to appreciate her flair for style, her creativity, her intelligence, and the sheer pleasure of being in her company. It was a joy to share plans and ideas with her. Together, she and my dad made a matchless couple.

Chris, you are gone now, and this is a desperately sad occasion. Your family and friends love and miss you so very much. May God bless you.

Old Headington
January 1998